BLACK OXFORD

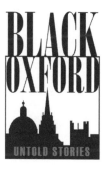

To Enid Roberts

BLACK OXFORD

The Untold Stories of
Oxford University's Black Scholars

PAMELA ROBERTS

Signal Books
Oxford

First published in 2013 by
Signal Books Limited
36 Minster Road
Oxford OX4 1LY
www.signalbooks.co.uk

A catalogue record for this book is available from the British Library

ISBN 978-1-908493-83-5 Paper

Cover Design: Tora Kelly
Typesetting: Tora Kelly
Cover Images: (front) By Kind Permission of Keble College, Oxford; (back) portrait of
Sir Hugh Springer by Hector Whistler by kind permission of the Warden and Fellows
of All Souls College, Oxford

Printed and bound in Great Britain by TJ International Ltd, Padstow, Cornwall

CONTENTS

AUTHOR'S PREFACE

The University of Oxford has existed since the twelfth century, and is universally regarded as one of Britain's - and the world's - top universities, having produced 26 British prime ministers, as well as many scientists, poets and famous writers. Countless books have been written about the University and its many alumni; but why is so little known specifically about its Black scholars?

I came to write this book as a result of a crude answer to a simple question. My question was this: with Oxford being a large multicultural city that attracts visitors from all over the world, were there any guided tours, similar to the walking tours operating in the city on a daily basis, which cast light on the history of Black scholars at the University?

The answer, from a local government officer, 'informed' me that Black people only arrived in the 1960s to drive the buses and work in the factories, and there was definitely no such history of Black scholars.

Now I know that many people, Black and white, may still be under the impression that the majority of Black people came to Britain in the late 1940s, a perception gained perhaps from anecdotal information and archival images of young Black men, women and children disembarking the gangway of SS Empire Windrush, which arrived at Tilbury on 22 June 1948, with 492 West Indian migrants, thus signalling the start of 'Britain's Black presence'. It is certainly true that organizations such as London Transport, British Rail, the National Health Service and the British Hotels and Restaurants Association all actively recruited workers in the Caribbean for the reconstruction of post-war England. However, this crude answer – and the idea that no Black history existed before - marked the beginning of a journey that would generate a major project and propel me to write this book.

The project, *Black Oxford: Untold Stories* was born; it consisted of the first guided heritage walking tour of the University, visiting a number of colleges, and a touring exhibition. The walking tour attracted a diverse audience among teachers, historians, students and families. A phone call from a parent who had recently completed the tour informed me that she then went to purchase a book on Oxford alumni; none of the scholars I had talked about on the tour featured in the book - or was even mentioned.

Thinking this could not be the case, I undertook my own research exercise. I visited Oxford's bookshops to look at the range of publications about the University and, more particularly, its famous alumni. I noted that not one book contained any information about nor a single image of Black scholars. The only references to other non-white scholars were to Aung San Suu Kyi of Burma, Prince Naruhito of Japan, Indira Gandhi of India or Benazir Bhutto of Pakistan.

The absence of any reference to Black scholars might lead you to assume that none had attended the University. It was almost as if they had been airbrushed out of the official history. Yet clearly this is not the case; the absence was all the more remarkable as I was delivering a walking tour highlighting a history of scholars who had travelled to the University from Africa, the United States, the Caribbean, South America and even Australia to study for Oxford degrees.

In researching and writing this book, I met many obstacles and barriers, but I also had some fascinating encounters or what I like to term 'adventures'. One such adventure was the quest to find out more about the first Black student of anthropology, James Arthur Harley.

The adventure began, quite unexpectedly, in New Zealand when I was on holiday, visiting a Maori heritage and culture centre in Rotorua. During a tour of the centre I mentioned to the guide the *Black Oxford* project. She looked at me nonplussed, and I assumed that she had not understood what I had said.

At the end of the tour the guide asked me to follow her to the gift shop, I thought to make me buy some kind of obligatory tourist knick-knack. Instead, she led me to the book section of the shop, removed a book and handed it to me, proudly announcing, 'this is Makereti, the first Maori woman to attend Oxford University.'

Reading the book I learnt that Makereti (1873-1930), also known as Maggie Papakura, was a true pioneer. Born to a Maori mother and British father, she worked from an early age in New Zealand's tourism industry, keen to explain all aspects of Maori

Maggie Papakura, photograph taken by William Henry Thomas Partington, c. 1910

culture to visitors. She led the Royal party of the Duke and Duchess of Cornwall and York around the famous Whakarewarewa geyser valley in 1901. Ten years later she brought a troupe of performers and a carved Maori village to the 1911 Festival of Empire at London's Crystal Palace. In 1927 she became a member of the Society of Oxford Home Students (which later evolved into St. Anne's College), a body that enabled women to study while living in private homes. Makereti was admitted to study anthropology.

She first lived in Oddington, a village outside Oxford, with her second husband Richard Staples-Browne, and then in Summertown, Oxford. She suffered from ill health and lack of money and died with her thesis unfinished. Makereti donated her large collection of Maori artefacts to the Pitt Rivers Museum, where a number of items are on display.

I contacted Jeremy Coote, curator of the Museum, to view the collection. It was while I was at the Pitt Rivers that Jeremy introduced me to Christopher Morton, Curator of Manuscripts and Photographs. Christopher handed me a sepia photograph, an image portraying four people, three men and one woman, in early Edwardian dress. Pointing to the Black man at the end of the photograph, Christopher asked, 'do you know anything about him?' 'No,' I replied. 'He's James Harley. All we know is that he came from Antigua and was the first Black student to take the Diploma of Anthropology at Pitt Rivers Museum in 1909.' I took a copy of the photograph, and after a quick Google search, which produced no information, I 'filed' the photograph.

In collating information for this book I was soon to be reacquainted with the sepia image. My starting point was that Harley came from Antigua, and so a letter quickly made its way to the High Commissioner for Antigua in London. The letter I received back contained six bullet points, one of which stated that Harley was a curate and lived in Shepshed, Leicestershire.

I though that there must be a local history group in Shepshed that might know of Harley, and after a series of phone calls, leading to a number of dead ends, I was put in touch with a local historian, who to my astonishment enthusiastically asked: 'you want to know about "Old Harley"?' My screeching of 'yes please' resulted in an invitation to visit the next day.

Michael and Margaret Wortley, a retired couple in their seventies, welcomed us into their home, and for some strange reason I had the feeling that I had known them for years, as we all chatted so easily like long lost friends - maybe because of our shared interest in Harley.

Michael explained that his father was handed a battered old suitcase after Harley's death in 1943. Upon his father's death, Michael and his sister cleared out their father's flat; his sister wanted to throw away the suitcase, but Michael, as a historian, insisted that it should be kept. Michael had brought the suitcase downstairs from under his bed - its usual place of residence - into the dining room in readiness for my visit, where it remained unopened. After all this time, from the first sight of the sepia photograph through the quest for further information, the opening of this suitcase felt like an occasion that should be marked by a glass of something alcoholic.

'Wow,' was the only word I could manage once the suitcase was opened. To say that Harley's life was in this case would be a considerable understatement; dusty pieces of papers pieced together Harley's fascinating career and offered some tantalising evidence on his lineage. His life is explored later in this book.

The writing of this book has taken me - and I am loath to use the reality television cliché - on a journey, but a journey of sorts it has been, both literal and emotional. It has included climbing the stone steps to gain access to the Keeper of the Archives at the Bodleian Library to view the leather bound ledgers of matriculation records, receiving emails from scholars or their families and being invited into their homes to view archive material and revisit their lives through photographs, certificates and their memories.

What this book sets out to illustrate is that Black scholars have been attending and succeeding at the University of Oxford since the turn of the twentieth century. It is not intended as an academic or comprehensive study of all such individuals who have attended the University, nor is it a meant to me a critique of the University's policy of attracting and admitting Black students.

It focuses on the late nineteenth century onwards, although archival records of all scholars' matriculation records and their exam results, dating back to 1507, exist at the Bodleian Library with the Keeper of the Archives. These, however, do not specify the ethnic origins of the scholars. The early records, in Latin, record each scholar's name, date and place of birth and father's position, categorized as Peer, Esquire, Gentleman, Cleric or Plebeian.

This book aims to serve as an introduction to some of the more famous as well as some lesser-known Black scholars, their lives, their impact, contributions and legacies. The Introduction therefore attempts only an outline explanation of how they came to study at Oxford, while the main text offers selected biographies of prominent figures, arranged by partly subject of study and eventual profession and partly by chronology.

I trust that you will find the profiles and careers of these scholars as interesting and inspiring as I have.

Pamela Roberts, 2013

GLOSSARY

The following are a number of terms used throughout the book that it may be useful to define for the reader.

A student unattached to any college or hall is referred to as a **non-collegiate student.**

A student who fulfils the required entry criteria for a specific undergraduate degree is **matriculated**, registered as an official student, with his or her name entered on the University's historic roll and becoming a member of the University for life. Students are formally admitted to membership of the University at the **matriculation ceremony.**

The University is headed by a **Chancellor and Vice-chancellor.** Each college has its own head, titles varying from college to college, e.g. Dean of Christ Church, Master of Balliol, Warden of New College.

The **Fellows** of a college are its senior members who make up the governing body. An **Honorary Fellow** is entitled to certain privileges but receives no payment and cannot share in the governing of the college. Many of the Black Oxford scholars became Honorary Fellows of their colleges or were elected to other colleges.

Encaenia Is the annual ceremony at the end of each academic year, which takes place in Trinity Term in the latter part of June, at which honorary degrees are conferred. The ceremony takes places in the Sheldonian Theatre, the proceedings are opened by the Chancellor, and each honouree is introduced by the Public Orator with a speech in Latin and admitted to his or her new degree by the Chancellor.

The **Junior Common Room** (JCR) is the formal undergraduate student organisation of a college and is the hub of undergraduate social activity as well as a physical location in a college for student recreation.

The **Oxford Union**, the world's most prestigious debating society, was founded in 1823 with the aim of promoting debate and discussion.

Phi Beta Kappa is America's oldest academic honour society. It honours students for the excellence and breadth of their scholarly accomplishment. An ideal Phi Beta Kappa has to demonstrate intellectual integrity, tolerance of other views and a broad range of academic interests.

Cum laude: graduating with honours; **magna cum laude**: graduating with great honours.

Gray's Inn, Lincoln's Inn and the **Inner Temple** are three of the four Inns of Court (professional associations for barristers and judges) in London. To be called to the Bar and practise as a barrister in England and Wales, an individual must belong to one of these Inns.

The Inner Temple Library by Herbert Railton, 1895

INTRODUCTION

'Towery city and branchy between towers;
Cuckoo-echoing, bell-swarmed, lark-charmed, rook-racked, river-rounded;
The dapple-eared lily below thee; that country and town did
Once encounter in, here coped and poised powers;'

The opening verse of Gerard Manley Hopkins' poem 'Duns Scotus's Oxford' paints an evocative image of Oxford as the quintessentially English city, coupled with one of the world's oldest universities with over 900 years of history and traditions. It is not a city or university that is usually associated with Black people, even in this day and age.

To many this archetypical view of Oxford still prevails, reinforced by many expressions of literature and other forms of culture; the image has certainly been replicated by successful television series such as *Brideshead Revisited, Inspector Morse, Lewis* and more recently *Endeavour*. These programmes are sold to worldwide audiences therefore providing the impetus for the perpetuation of the stereotype.

The city does, however, have a diverse population, with immigration dating back over the centuries. The Black community can trace its presence back to the sixteenth century, partly through Oxfordshire's involvement in slavery. In

'City of dreaming spires', c. 1890

the twentieth century industry and an expanding public sector attracted people from around the world, including established communities of African and Caribbean origins. Today there are significant numbers of Oxford residents with African or Caribbean backgrounds. The focus of this book, however, is not about the Black presence in the city; it is about the many Black students who came to study at its famous university.

Although no clear date is agreed for the foundation of the University of Oxford, teaching of some form existed by 1096, developing rapidly after Henry II banned English students from attending the University of Paris. In the thirteenth century, after so-called 'town and gown' conflict between the city's residents and students, the University encouraged the establishment of early halls of residence. These became the first of Oxford's colleges, which were endowed houses under the supervision of a master; the oldest are University, Balliol and Merton Colleges, established between 1249 and 1264.

The University's tradition of international scholarly links began with the arrival of a student from the Netherlands, Emo of Friesland, the first known overseas student, in 1190. Young Africans were sent to Europe for education, one notable example was the son of the King of the Congo, who studied in Portugal. There then developed a sequence of such migrations to British schools and universities from Africa and the Caribbean, when African rulers and the mission-educated African elite, especially in towns like Freetown, Lagos and Accra along the coast of West Africa, commonly sent their children abroad to gain a British education, as did prominent West Indian families.

In the United States, the establishment of Historically Black Colleges and Universities (HBCUs) afforded Black students the chance of a university education, and although some attended the Ivy League universities of Harvard, Yale, Pennsylvania, Princeton, Columbia, Brown, Dartmouth or Cornell, many still chose to apply for a British education at the University of Oxford.

The opportunity to attend a university in the Caribbean, Guyana or Africa (with the exception of Fourah Bay College, University of Sierra Leone, established in 1827) simply did not exist until the twentieth century. The first institutions founded in the Caribbean and Guyana were the University of the West Indies in 1948 and the University of Guyana in 1963. Universities in Africa began in 1908 with the University of Egypt, followed by the Universities of Uganda (1922), Kenya (1939), Ghana and Nigeria (1948), Ethiopia, Zimbabwe, Mozambique and Angola (1950s-1980s).

For many students an academic place in Britain had represented the only option for professional degrees. In attempting to apply for the University of Oxford, Black students knew they would be attending a renowned seat of learning, with its reputation as one of the best universities in the world.

The Route to Oxford

The route to Oxford for many Black students followed an established path: attending a noted grammar school in their home country, successfully completing their school education and applying for a scholarship. This could be either a Rhodes Scholarship or their own country's scholarship, for example, from Trinidad-Tobago, Barbados, Jamaica or Guyana. Known as the Colonial Scholarship or Exhibition, the latter awarded a place at Oxford, Cambridge or Edinburgh; the Rhodes Scholarship was solely for Oxford.

Some of the students who came to Oxford in the nineteenth century would have attended one of the schools established by the Church Missionary Society (CMS), or another charity. One of these charities was the Mico Foundation (originally the Lady Mico Charity), established by Sir Samuel Mico, an English trader who died in 1666, leaving his wealth to his wife, Lady Jane Mico, and his nephew Samuel. The charity established 300 elementary schools in the British colonies of the West Indies.

The Caribbean, Guyana and Africa had their share of elite schools, just as England did, including Jamaica College in Jamaica, Queen's College in Trinidad, Codrington College and Harrison College in Barbados, Queen's College and

Buxton House, Mico University College, Jamaica

Bishop's High School in Guyana, Fourah Bay College in Sierra Leone and Achimota School in Ghana. The majority of these schools followed the same curricula and methods that were used in British public schools, including the use of British textbooks and examinations. The guiding principle of the colonial education system was the traditional British view that the purpose of the best secondary education was to prepare the elite for its role in society.

Looking at each of these institutions in more detail: the Queen's College Grammar School for Boys in Guyana, formerly British Guiana, was established in 1844 by the Most Reverend William Piercy Austin, DD, Bishop of British Guiana. From its inception, a prestigious secondary school in the capital, Georgetown, the school was open to all, irrespective of colour, race, creed or social position; however, entry to the school was mainly dependent on the payment of fees, which then were G$80 per year. The intention of the founder was to provide scholarships and exhibitions to enable deserving students to take up study in British universities. The academic curriculum was based on that of King's College London; after students had studied classics, mathematics and modern languages, scholarships or exhibitions were to be awarded to Oxford and Cambridge.

Charles Drax, a planter originally from England who came to Jamaica from Barbados in 1721, founded Jamaica College in 1795 in the parish of St. Ann. The fourth oldest high school in the country, it was first known as the Drax Free School, after Dax left money in his will to establish a charity school. From 1903 the sole purpose of Jamaica College was to train potential university students.

With a *raison d'être* of turning young Trinidadians into young English gentlemen, Queen's Royal College in Trinidad, originally Queen's Collegiate School, was set up as the apex of the secular educational system, established in an ordinance of 1859. The college provided a classical education in mathematics, Latin, Greek, French, German, English language and literature, English history and geography. The type of curriculum offered at Queen's College set a pattern for the whole secondary school system in Trinidad.

The Eton of Barbados was the description given to Harrison College, as it was recognized as perhaps the most prestigious secondary school in the British West Indies. Originally an all boys grammar school, situated in Bridgetown, it was founded in 1733, by Thomas Harrison, a Bridgetown merchant, who intended it to serve as 'A Public and Free School for the poor and indigent boys of the parish'. The school later introduced co-education with girls admitted into the sixth form in 1977 and the lower forms two years later.

Codrington College was named after its benefactor Christopher Codrington, a Christ Church alumnus and an elected fellow of All Souls College, Oxford. He bequeathed his slave plantations to the Society for the Propagation of the Gospel in Foreign Parts, for the foundation of a college in Barbados. Built between 1715 and 1743 and officially opened in 1745, it was essentially a theological college to train West Indian ministers. Codrington also bequeathed a legacy of £10,000 to All Souls College in 1710, to buy books worth £4,000 and build the Codrington Library.

Within the continent of Africa, Fourah Bay College in Sierra Leone stands as one of the oldest institutions of higher education, with an academic reputation

School fete, Codrington College, c. 1850

which extended throughout West Africa. It was founded in 1827 by the Church Missionary Society, essentially for the training of teachers and missionaries to serve in the promotion of education and the spread of Christianity in West Africa. In 1876 it became a degree-granting institution, with an affiliation to the University of Durham in England, and since then has maintained a reputable tradition of higher education in Africa. In 1960 it was granted a Royal Charter to become 'Fourah Bay College, the University College of Sierra Leone' by the Senate of the University of Durham.

Liberia College was founded in 1863 as a school and became a university in 1951. Fort Hare in the Eastern Cape was founded in 1916, under the name of the South African Native College. In Uganda, Makerere, founded in 1922 as a technical college, became University College Makerere in 1949; affiliated to London University it achieved independent university status in 1970. In the Congo, Lovanium College was established in 1949, although no students were admitted until 1954. In Nigeria, Ibadan University was opened in 1948, also affiliated to London University.

Founded by three forward-thinking ideologists - Sir Frederick Gordon Guggisberg, Dr. James Emman Kwegyir Aggrey and Reverend Alexander Garden Fraser, Achimota School, formerly Prince of Wales College and School, was established in 1924 and commenced operations in 1927. An elite and highly selective co-educational secondary school, it is located at Achimota in Accra, Ghana.

Inauguration of Achimota School, 1927

The founders' radical ambition was to create a school that would be a model for all of West Africa - a school that would educate Ghanaian boys and girls so well that they would be completely at ease in both traditional culture and Western settings. Their vision extended to producing a class of intellectually bi-cultural leaders whose training would enable them to act as interpreters and brokers for European and African ideas, fully able to take over their country's government when the time inevitably came for the British to leave. The school has educated many African leaders, including Kwame Nkrumah and Jerry John Rawlings, both of whom are former Heads of State of Ghana. Former Black Oxford scholars Edward Akufo-Addo and Prime Minister Dr. Kofi Abrefa Busia taught at Achimota.

Wesleyan, Methodist, Anglican and Catholic missionaries brought Western-style education to the Gambia by establishing schools in the country's capital city, Bathurst (later renamed Banjul) in the early nineteenth century. The Wesleyan Mission arrived in 1824, invited by the Governor, Sir Charles McCarthy. The Mission established the Wesleyan Boys High School in 1876. The school changed its name and re-opened as the Methodist Boys' High School in 1898. The Methodist Girls' High School was opened much later in 1915. The school is now known as The Gambia Senior Secondary School.

In America, the history of education for Black children has its origins in slavery, civil war and reconstruction. Before the civil war (1861-65) the majority of Blacks in the United States were enslaved. Although a few free Blacks attended mainly white colleges in the North in the years before the war, such opportunities were very rare, and non-existent in the slave states of the South. The Historically Black Colleges and Universities (HBCU) were 'invented' in 1837, 26 years before the end of slavery. Tortola-born Richard Humphreys (1750-1832), a Quaker philanthropist, founded the Institute for Colored Youth to train free Blacks to become teachers. His will instructed Quaker executors 'to instruct the descendents of the African Race in school learning, in the various branches of the mechanic Arts, trades and Agriculture, in order to prepare and fit and qualify them to act as teachers.' This institution has the earliest founding date of an HBCU, although for most of its early history it offered only elementary and high-school-level instruction. In 1902 the school moved from Philadelphia to Cheyney, where it eventually became Cheyney University.

Booker T. Washington

Between 1861 and 1870 the American Missionary Association (AMA) founded seven Black colleges and thirteen inclusive teaching schools. Many of these institutions, along with the private Historically Black Colleges and Universities, became the backbone of Black higher education, producing African-American leaders for generations to come.

Two leaders and graduates from the first generation of students to attend these new Black institutions, Booker T. Washington and W. E. B. Dubois, had different views of the course Black colleges should take. Washington, a freed slave from Virginia, attended the Hampton Normal and Agricultural Institute. Hampton's focus was on preparing young Blacks throughout the South to fill jobs in the skilled trades. In 1881 Washington took charge at the new Tuskegee Institute in Alabama. Tuskegee quickly became noted for delivering a practical curriculum and preparing Blacks for many agricultural and mechanical trades.

Taking a radically different approach to Washington's universal vocational training, Dubois dismissed such training as only reinforcing stereotypical images and perpetuating the servitude of slavery. Dubois' approach as to how

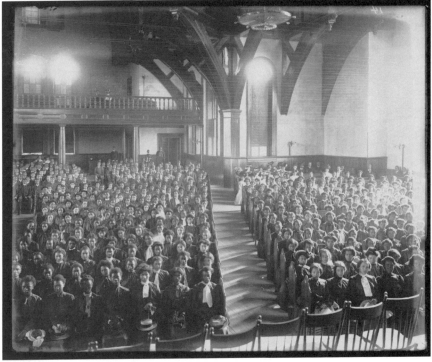

Tuskegee Institute, 1902

Black people should progress in society brought him into open conflict with Washington. Raised in Massachusetts and first exposed to segregation during his undergraduate work at Fisk University in Nashville, Tennessee, Dubois was a fierce advocate of civil rights; he believed that it was essential that Blacks receive training not only in vocational fields, but also in the liberal arts, and that talented Blacks could become teachers and leaders if they were allowed to study the arts and sciences.

By 1902 at least 85 schools were set up by white philanthropists, free Blacks, states or churches to educate sons and daughters of former slaves.

W. E. B. Dubois, 1918

Historically Black Colleges and Universities were the number one option for most Blacks interested in attending college. Today there are more than a hundred such HBCUs in the United States, some of the most notable being Tuskegee, Fisk, Howard, Spelman and Moorehouse. The HBCUs have evolved dramatically since 1837 when their objective was to educate freed slaves to read and write.

Scholarships

In the Caribbean, a system of state scholarships for gifted pupils who could not afford to continue their education was developed in the late nineteenth century. The Island Scholarship, also known as the Colonial Scholarship, was administered by the local colonial governor. One scholarship was awarded annually, the selection criteria being based on the Oxford and Cambridge Higher School Certificate, or the University of London Higher School Certificate.

The Guiana Scholarship was established in June 1881, when the governor resolved that three Colonial Scholarships to a university in the United Kingdom be awarded each year. A committee appointed in 1883 considered suggestions about the examinations for the Guiana Scholarships. It recommended that the test examination should be the Cambridge Local Senior Examination, the qualification being at least second class honours or third class honours with distinction.

The value of the scholarship was £600, spread over three or four years, tenable at a British university or an Inn of Court. The age limit was nineteen at the commencement of the examination. The holder of the scholarship was entitled to a free passage to England, and also to a free return passage to their colony, if they satisfied the governor that they intended to take up residence in the colony. In 1890 two scholarships were awarded, one going to the first 'coloured' boy to win the scholarship; and in 1894 the only candidate to obtain first class honours was the first Black to win the scholarship.

The Guiana and Island Scholarships provided hitherto unavailable opportunities; in particular, it was noted that they gave Black scholars the ability to progress further than if they had stayed in their own country, perhaps only achieving a senior level in the civil service.

In Africa, scholarships remained scarce: the opportunity to pursue higher education depended on the student's ability to marshal financial support. The average age of scholars from the Gold Coast during the last decade of the nineteenth century was 31, suggesting that many had to work for years to save the required funds.

One of the principal means that enabled a large number of Black scholars to attend Oxford University at the turn of the century was the Rhodes Scholarship. Educated at Bishop Stortford Grammar School, Cecil John Rhodes (1853-1902) attended Oriel College and earned his Master of Arts degree in 1881 after a long period from 1873 when he was only intermittently in Oxford. He was not a model student, according to his tutor A. G. Butler: 'His career at Oxford was uneventful. He belonged to a set of men like himself, not caring for distinction in the schools [examinations] and not working for them,

'The Rhodes Colossuss', *Punch* 10 December 1892

but of refined tastes, dining and living for the most part together, and doubtless discussing passing events in life and politics with interest and ability.' His academic life was interspersed with business adventures. He obtained a large interest in the newly worked Kimberley diamond mines and amalgamated then into the De Beers Consolidated Mines amassing a multi-million-pound fortune in gold and diamonds. He was to become known as an advocate of British imperialism in Africa, a magnate and the founder of Rhodesia.

The Rhodes Scholarships, administered by the Rhodes Trust, are the feature of Rhodes' sixth and final will, drawn up in 1899 at the age of forty-six. Rhodes' vision for world peace was expressed in his financing of the Rhodes Scholars, to educate future leaders of the world by allowing them to study for three years at Oxford University. Scholars drawn from the British Commonwealth, the United States and Germany would then return to their countries, theoretically to prevent the First World War, which he feared likely to happen, and which did of course take place between 1914 and 1918. To mark the 25th anniversary of the Scholarships in 1928, Rhodes Trustees built Rhodes House, a colonial-style building on South Parks Road, to serve as both a home for the Rhodes Trust

Rhodes House

and the Scholarships, and as a memorial to Rhodes himself. Rhodes House now contains the Bodleian Library of Commonwealth and African Studies, part of the University's library collection.

Cecil Rhodes laid down the following criteria by which Rhodes Scholars were to be selected:

Thirty per cent for literary and scholastic attainments;
Twenty per cent for fondness for and success in manly outdoor sports, such as cricket, football and the like;
Thirty per cent for qualities of truth, courage, devotion to duty, sympathy for and protection of the weak, kindliness, unselfishness and fellowship;
Twenty per cent for exhibiting during their school days signs of moral force of character and instincts to lead and take an interest in their schoolmates.

Rhodes chose to endow these postgraduate scholarships at Oxford because he believed 'Its residential colleges provided an environment especially conductive to personal development'. His view was unashamedly elitist: 'Wherever you turn your eye - except in science - an Oxford man is at the top of the tree.'

Established in 1903, the Rhodes Scholarships is the oldest and, arguably, the most prestigious international graduate scholarship programme in the world. Alain LeRoy Locke became the first Black to be awarded a Rhodes Scholarship in 1907.

The early Rhodes Scholars received £300 a year, having reached Oxford without the Trust's financial assistance. From this stipend they paid their fees and living expenses. Scholarships were originally awarded for three years, which was then the minimum time for obtaining an Oxford degree. Today scholarships are awarded for two years.

Rhodes Scholars have their fares and baggage costs paid in each direction, and have their college and University fees paid directly by the Trust, as well as receiving an annual stipend of £12,516 (as of 2011).

Women were not eligible to apply for Rhodes Scholarships as the interpretation of the will, by the Rhodes Trust Acts of Parliament, confined the awards to male students only. No women were awarded Rhodes Scholarships until 1977, when the Sex Discrimination Act of 1976 made it illegal for the scholarship to be only applicable to men. The first Black female Rhodes Scholar, Karen Stevenson, matriculated at Oxford in 1979.

The distribution of Rhodes Scholarships, as of 2011, is as follows:

United States	32
Canada	11
South Africa	8
Australia	9
India	5
Germany	2
Zambia and Zimbabwe	4
New Zealand	3
Kenya	2
Commonwealth Caribbean	1
Bermuda	1
Jamaica	1
Pakistan	1
Hong Kong	1
BLMNS (Botswana, Lesotho, Malawi, Namibia, and Swaziland)	1

Women at Oxford

As an exclusively white upper- and middle-class male bastion of privilege and opportunity, the establishment of the University could not foresee women entering its esteemed colleges and undertaking an academic course of study or - much worse - university examinations. However, in 1879 twenty-one pioneering women entered two recently established residential halls - the emerging colleges of Lady Margaret Hall and Somerville.

Women's colleges came to be established as a result of the pioneering work of the Association for Promoting the Higher Education of Women (AEW). Lady Margaret Hall and Somerville opened in 1879, followed by St. Hugh's in 1886 and St. Hilda's in 1893. St. Anne's, which in 1952 was the last of the women's colleges to be incorporated by Royal Charter, originated as the Society of Oxford Home Students.

Although women had attended lectures, taken examinations and had gained honours in those examinations from the late 1870s they were unable to receive the degree to which their examinations would have entitled them. The new University statute of 1920, which came into effect from October of that year, admitted women to full membership of the University. This enabled women, who had previously taken and gained honours in University examinations, to return to matriculate and have the degree to which they were now entitled conferred on them. Full collegiate status was conferred on the five women's societies in 1959.

The first intake of students at Lady Margaret Hall, October 1879

Oxford University Today

The University of Oxford now comprises 38 colleges and six permanent private halls. It is the colleges which largely determine their own admissions policies. In 2012 the colleges accepted a total of 32 Black students for undergraduate courses, the highest number in ten years, by comparison with 27 Black students in 2009. The 2012 figure represents an acceptance rate of 14 per cent, compared with 8.8 per cent the previous year, when the acceptance rate for white students was 24.1 per cent. Only in 2008 did the Oxford Students' Union elect its first Black president: Lewis Iwu from East London, destined for a career in law.

OXFORD PIONEERS

'Oxford is a training-school for the governing classes, and has taught your son a lesson.' Alain LeRoy Locke, letter to his mother.

CHRISTIAN FREDERICK COLE, 1852-85
University College

Barrister and the first African to practise law in an English court

Christian Frederick Cole was the second son of Jacob Cole of Kissy, and the adopted son of the Rev. James Cole of Waterloo, Sierra Leone. He enrolled at University College, Oxford as a non-collegiate student in 1873, aged twenty-one.

Cole chose to read for an honours degree in classics, which cannot have been easy; his status as a non-collegiate student indicates that he was poor. To supplement his income, Cole, a talented musician, taught music lessons, advertised in the *Oxford University Gazette*, a weekly journal of the University. He also taught 'Responsions', the first of the three examinations once required for an academic degree at the University, as well as preparing students for the divinity examination, which they had to pass to graduate. From accounts he attracted many students to his classes, maybe at first because he was viewed as a curio, but he was very popular. He achieved a fourth in Greats in 1876. In November 1877 he was accepted as a member of University College.

Cole made a point of attending Encaenia. The *Oxford Chronicle* of 29 June 1878 noted that, before the Encaenia procession entered, 'Some amusement was caused by "Three Cheers for Christian Cole", a gentleman of colour, of University College, who had entered the Theatre a few moments previously and was standing in the area.' He remained a member of college until April 1880.

There were obvious elements of racism in some reactions to Cole. Anna Florence Ward, whose brother William was a close friend of Oscar Wilde, noted in her diary entry relating to the annual Show Sunday Promenade in the Broad Walk, Christ Church, on 18 June 1876: 'Saw Cole (Coal?) also (the nigger).' Cole also attracted the attention of contemporary cartoonists of the day, and two images of him were reproduced(see next page), which would be viewed as racist stereotypes today. One illustrates Cole being parachuted into 'an African village' dressed in a grass skirt. The image notes that he received the rather unoriginal nickname of 'Old King Cole'. What Cole thought of these cartoons, and all the comments passed on him, is not known. We do know, however, that he chose to live up to them by playing as visible a part in university life as he could.

Cole returned home to Sierra Leone after obtaining his degree, but could not find any employment there. He delivered a series of lectures that were published

2

Contemporary cartoon of Christian Frederick Cole

at Freetown in 1880 under the title 'Education'. He also published a slim pamphlet of two poems titled *Reflections on the Zulu War. By a Negro, B.A., of University College, Oxford, and the Inner Temple*, price three pence. This little book is very rare: a copy was found for sale on the internet costing over £1,000. Three Oxford college archivists clubbed together to purchase the booklet, which is now in University College library.

Frustrated at home, Cole returned to England to qualify for the Bar. He was called to the Inner Temple in 1883, and became the first Black African to practise in the English courts. Cole then moved to East Africa to work as a barrister there. But unfortunately he died of smallpox in 1885 in Zanzibar, when he was just 33 years old.

Reflections on the Zulu War
By a Negro, B.A., of University College, Oxford,
and the Inner Temple,

The Future of Africa
Dedicated to Bishop Colenso and looked forward to a time when Africans
Will with stunning pride asserts their claims
And put to silence all opprobrious names.
The world with eyes wide open shall then exclaim
Afric! Thy sons have won eternal fame.

LADY KOFOWOROLA ABENI ADEMOLA, 1913-2002
St. Hugh's College

Educator and the first African woman to receive a degree from the University

The first African woman to be awarded a degree at Oxford was Kofoworola (Kofo) Moore, a Yoruba born in Lagos, Nigeria, on 21 May 1913. Her parents, the Honourable Eric Olawolu Moore CBE and Mrs. Arabella Aida Moore, and her grandfather had all been educated in England. Her father was a lawyer of distinguished reputation, a barrister-at-law, who practised law in Lagos. He was a member of the Legislative Council, and was awarded a CBE by the government for services to his nation.

Kofoworola was rather delicate as a young child. She began school after her third birthday and attended kindergarten at the CMS Girls' Seminary, later proceeding to the primary school. Friends and contemporaries remember her as 'very fair, very pretty and very friendly'. Her childhood was marred by frequent illnesses, and she was congratulated by her teachers if she managed to attend school for a month at a stretch. She was plagued by recurring malaria, and a severe bout of illness in 1923 made her mother decide that the climate in England might be less damaging to her health. >Ademola tif<

She attended Portway College in Reading to complete her schooling. Kofoworola wanted to develop a career in education, in particular teaching. However, her father had different ideas. Kofoworola said: 'My father wanted me to study law because he himself is a barrister with a practice established over thirty years, and I would have been sure of a good beginning. Also, there would have been the prestige of being the second lady barrister in West Africa.' Not in favour of his daughter's preference for teaching, he presented Kofoworola with a proposal: prior to starting teacher training she was to try for a place at either Oxford or Cambridge. A place was offered to Kofoworola at St. Hugh's College to read English, so she attended St. Hugh's from 1932 to 1935.

At first she was unhappy and bewildered at Oxford: 'I never felt as out of place and as homesick in England as I felt in the first two weeks at Oxford. I seemed tossed in a sea of intellect with highly earnest students who were themselves occupied in trying to emerge from the surging whirl… but gradually I discovered that we were all aground on dry land and I was among a sympathetic crowd.'

She found herself in a group of friends from various countries reading different subjects, whose common ground was music. She joined the Labour Club, the African Society and the English Club. Kofoworola received more invitations to coffee parties in her first two terms than the number received by all the first year students.

> What is far more exasperating than the more acute form of colour prejudice is being regarded as a 'curio' or some weird specimen of nature's product, not as an ordinary human being; and of that I have experience. I recall being taken to tea with a lady who had never met an African before. After the first introduction she coolly told me, in a tone of relief which, however, failed to hide her disappointment that I was not what she expected. For the rest of the time with her she ejaculated 'How very interesting!' at the end of all the remarks I made; I believe she even said 'How very interesting!' when I was saying 'Goodbye'.

Summing up her ideas and impressions about Oxford, Kofoworola said in her autobiography, 'They would be expressed in the wish that there could be at least two African girl scholars in Oxford each year.'

She married Sir Adetokunbo Ademola, a Cambridge graduate who became Chief Justice of Nigeria in 1955. She co-founded Oriel Girls' School, Lagos, and was tutor and headmistress at different times at Queen's College, Lagos, the foremost government secondary college for girls at that time. Her position gave

Lady Kofoworola Moore, centre, in traditional African dress

her the opportunity to encourage girls to work to the best of their ability. She told them: 'Brains have no sex; you can do as well and even better than some boys. You have brains too.'

An active member in a number of women's organizations, Kofoworola was made a Member of the Order of the British Empire (MBE) for her work with the Red Cross. She received the honour personally from Queen Elizabeth, the Queen Mother, on her visit to England in 1959. Kofoworola was also made an Officer of the Federal Republic (OFR) by Prime Minister Tafawa Balewa's administration. In her later life, Lady Ademola devoted her time to writing children's books. She died aged 89, after a brief illness.

St. Hugh's College

GEORGE FREDERICK HALL, 1891-1972
Lincoln College

Engineer and Queensland's first Black Rhodes Scholar

The son of a runaway slave and an immigrant mother, George Frederick Emanuel Hall was born on 19 October 1891 at Charters Towers, Queensland, Australia. His father, a runaway slave, was born in 1850 in the Caribbean island of Tobago and jumped ships to reach Australia, finally settling in Charters Towers, where he worked as a carter in the goldfields. His mother, Annie Elizabeth, née Collett, an English immigrant, was born in Wiltshire in 1863. Given his mother's age (she was 23 when she married Hall's father, who was 56), it is believed – though it is not conclusive - that she may have travelled to Australia as part of the 'Bounty scheme', one of the many early immigration schemes to encourage young couples and single women, who were paid £8, to start a new life in New South Wales.

The couple had six children, of whom George was the third. In 1897, at the age of five years and three months, George was enrolled at Richmond Hill State School, Charters Towers, as the school's 128th pupil. At the University of Sydney Junior Examination, Hall attained 6 As and 2 Bs. It was the best pass

Charters Towers, 1893

achieved by a boy from a Queensland school that year. Hall received a state bursary to study at Townsville Grammar School as a boarder in 1905.

A talented and gifted athlete, he became the school's cricket captain, senior gymnast, an outstanding footballer, shooter and swimmer as well as athletics champion three years in a row. He was the school's best scholar in 1909 as 'dux', the term given to the top student in academic and sporting achievement in each graduating year, and in the years 1909-10 was head prefect.

In 1909 Hall won the school's Rugby Prize, which was awarded annually on the joint vote of masters and boys 'to the boy who, in addition to holding a high position in the school through his work in form, has done good service in the athletic life of the school and exhibited honourable powers of leadership'.

P. F. Rowland, the Townsville Grammar School headmaster, offered these words as he presented Hall with the Governor's Cup for good service: 'The voting for this year's Rugby Prize took place yesterday, 8 December 1909. Every vote in the school was cast for Hall, except two, one of which I believe was Hall himself. It is a record over which any boy might well be proud. He has triumphed over prejudice by sheer merit; whatever will be his future, he can always look back on his years with us as years of success; whatever he does, he will carry with him the hearty good wishes of all at the school.'

In March 1910 Hall was elected Queensland's Rhodes Scholar for that year. The record shows that Hall came top of the class in all four categories. By being elected seventh Rhodes Scholar, Hall not only circumvented any systemic shortcomings but had the door to the world beyond Queensland and Australia opened for him.

The £300 scholarship entitled him to enter Lincoln College, Oxford. As the Rhodes Trust made no provision for the passage to Oxford, some Charters Towers businessmen raised the sum of £30 for his fare. This amount was also supplemented by £40 on behalf of the Old Boys' Union, along with a travelling rug.

The *North Queensland Register* in July 1910 reports on the town's presentation to George Hall:

> At Messrs E. D. Miles and Co's office on Tuesday afternoon, a modest but very pleasing presentation was made by Mr. J. Millican, on behalf of some of the Charters Towers citizens to our North Queensland Rhodes Scholar, Mr. George Hall, who left for Townsville yesterday morning on his way South to catch the Orient Co's steamer 'Orsova' on his way to Oxford University. In making the presentation, Mr. Millican said:
>
> 'It afforded him a very special pleasure to be requested to act on this

occasion; as he had know the father of George Hall for a large number of years, as a thoroughly good citizen, and a very straightforward man, and he was pleased to note that the son in these respects, gave evidence of desiring to follow in his father footsteps.

'He congratulated Mr. George Hall on his success, which was very creditable to himself and a source of satisfaction and pride to the resident of Charters Towers'.

Hall matriculated at Lincoln College to read medicine. In a letter to Townsville Grammar School, he wrote that he had passed his first year examinations in botany and zoology. This, however, did not deter him from changing subjects, choosing to read engineering science. He graduated with a second class honours degree in 1913. An accomplished cricketer, he was a member of Lincoln's First XI.

Hall then found employment with the Scottish firm of Andrew Barclay & Sons, which manufactured industrial locomotives. At the age of 26 he became a pilot when he enlisted in the Royal Air Force on 10 May 1918. When the war ended he was repatriated the following year to Australia in April 1919 as a second lieutenant.

After working with the New South Wales Cement, Lime & Coal Co. at Kandos, Hall moved to Sydney to begin a thirty-year working association with the Main Roads Board of New South Wales. Starting as an assistant engineer, he was promoted to the status of acting Class 2 Engineer in 1928. Hall had a team of engineers working under him at Milson Point, the north side of the Sydney Harbour Bridge. He eventually became a supervising engineer dealing with 31 municipal councils in the greater Sydney area.

G. F. E. Hall, Queensland Rhodes Scholar, 1910

According to the *Australian Dictionary of Biography*, 'covert racism was evident in Hall's sluggish promotion through the engineering ranks at the department, despite his colleagues believing him capable of greater things. He was a handsome man, of medium height, but he told workmates that, because his "ancestry would be a barrier", he decided never to marry.'

He retired as supervising engineer at the age of 65 in 1957. He died on 15 July 1972 at Parramatta District Hospital, Sydney, at the age of eighty, from a cerebral haemorrhage. He was cremated with Anglican rites. Memories of Hall's life and achievements are preserved by the Townsville Grammar School; his portrait takes pride of place in the school's foyer, and in his honour the girls' boarding school is named after him.

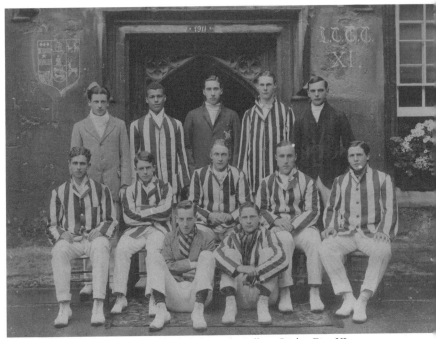

George Hall (back row, second left) in the Lincoln College Cricket First XI

ALAIN LEROY LOCKE, 1885-1954
Hertford College

Educator, artist and father of the Harlem Renaissance

A ground breaking pioneer, Alain LeRoy Locke became the first African-American Rhodes Scholar in 1907. Locke was born in 1885 into a distinguished Philadelphia family with interests in education and culture. His grandfather, Ishmael Locke, was a free African-American and teacher. The Society of Friends (Quakers) had sponsored his attending Cambridge University in England for higher education, after which Ishmael spent four years in Liberia establishing schools. Returning to the United States, he became headmaster of a school in Providence, Rhode Island, and then principal of the Institute for Colored Youth in Philadelphia. Alain's father, Pliny Ishmael Locke, graduated from the Institute in 1867, then taught mathematics there for two years before leaving to teach newly freed African-Americans in North Carolina.

Locke's early childhood had been marred when a severe bout of rheumatic fever permanently damaged his heart and restricted his physical activities. The illness, however, provided him with the opportunity to spend his time reading books and learning to play the piano and violin.

A graduate of the Central High School, in 1902, Locke went on to study at the Philadelphia School of Pedagogy, where he moved up to first in his class. Entering Harvard University, he studied under William James and some of the other leading American philosophers in the faculty.

William Carl Bolivar, a Philadelphia African-American journalist wrote in 1902 that:

> It was a remarkable achievement for anyone; not to mention an African-American during this highly segregated era - while many white American scholars were seeking to prove the intellectual inferiority of African-Americans to justify racial segregation, Locke became a symbol of achievement and a powerful argument for offering African-Americans equal opportunity at white educational institutions.

Locke completed Harvard's four-year programme in three, graduating *magna cum laude* with his bachelor's degree in philosophy in 1907, and was elected to Phi Beta Kappa.

Locke won Harvard's most prestigious award, the Bowdoin Prize, for an essay in English: 'The Literary Heritage of Tennyson'. It carried with it a medal, a public presentation of a thesis and $250. For the Rhodes Scholarship, he passed

11

BLACK OXFORD

SCHOOL OF PEDAGOGY
OF THE
CITY OF PHILADELPHIA
BROAD AND GREEN STREETS
FOUNDED 1891

(7)

March 7, 1901.

To the Committee on Rhodes' Scholarships,

Philadelphia.

Gentlemen:-

I wish to commend to your favorable consideration in the strongest possible terms Mr. Alain LeRoy Locke, a Philadelphian now a student at Harvard University, who has qualified for appointment to a Rhodes' Scholarship. Mr. Locke was graduated from the School of Pedagogy in June 1904 at the head of his class. His record in this school throughout two years shows him to have been a student of exceptional ability and promise, and a young gentleman of the finest instincts and highest character. I am convinced that Mr. Locke is a type of man who would profit in the highest degree by the opportunity for study at Oxford.

I should like respectfully to suggest that in the case of Mr. Locke the Committee has a rare opportunity to give recognition to a type of man which, for scholarship, gentlemanly qualities, and promise of usefulness, is likely never to have a better representative than Mr. Locke.

Yours very truly,

Francis Burke Brandt

Director of the School of Pedagogy.

12

the qualifying examination in Latin, Greek and mathematics, scoring the highest mark and beating seven white students in the process.

He was awarded the Scholarship before the committee discovered he was Black, but after careful consideration the committee decided to let the award stand. The Rhodes Scholarship provided for study at Oxford, but it was no guarantee of admission. Locke was rejected by five Oxford colleges because of his race before being accepted by Hertford College.

Locke made history and headlines in May 1907 as America's first African-American Rhodes Scholar, and the only one until the 1960s. He studied philosophy, Greek and Literae Humaniores.

At Oxford, he often went to the theatre and took piano lessons. The criteria for a Rhodes Scholarships required both athletic and academic skills and Locke

was no athlete. Even so, he took up rowing and won his rowing cap; he wrote to his mother: 'Every afternoon, rain or shine, I am out with the crew on the river.' Locke joined the French club and founded the Oxford Cosmopolitan Club, a group of international students, of which Pixley Seme (see p.51n) was Treasurer. He and Seme often went riding together, spoke French and together they founded the African Union Society.

A racial incident took place over a Thanksgiving Day dinner, hosted at the American Club, a dinner to which Locke was not invited because, according to his friend Horace Kallen, of some 'gentlemen from Dixie who could not possibly associate with Negroes'. These Southern Rhodes Scholars even appealed to the Rhodes trustees to withdraw Locke's award. The incident acutely traumatised Locke so that he left Oxford without taking his degree and spent the 1910-11 academic years studying the work of the German philosopher Immanuel Kant at the University of Berlin and touring Eastern Europe.

Locke returned to the United States, where was appointed an assistant professor of English at Howard University in Washington, DC. In the spring of 1911 Locke travelled with Booker T. Washington throughout the racist Deep South. As a direct result of his experiences with racism in the South, Locke resolved to promote the interests of African-Americans, using culture as a strategy. He also set about establishing Howard as the country's pre-eminent African-American university, a training ground for African-American intellectuals and a centre for African-American culture and research on racial problems. Meanwhile, he completed a PhD in Philosophy at Harvard in 1918.

Having studied African culture and traced its influences upon Western civilisation, he urged Black painters, sculptors and musicians to look to African sources for identity and to discover materials and techniques for their work. He encouraged Black authors to seek subjects in Black life and to set high artistic standards for themselves.

The burgeoning movement, which became known the Harlem Renaissance, started to flourish during the 1920s and 1930s, producing artists such as Langston Hughes, Zora Neale Hurston, Florence Mills and Aaron Douglas. Credited with being the father of the movement, Locke's underlying concept was that African-American literature, art and music could challenge racism, and promote social integration.

Locke familiarized American readers with the Harlem Renaissance by editing a special Harlem issue of *Survey Graphic* (March 1925), which he expanded into *The New Negro* (1925), an anthology of fiction, poetry, drama and essays. The Harlem Renaissance had an impact

Zora Neale Hurston

14

on cities across the United States, laying the foundations for the Civil Rights Movement.

Locke remained at Howard until retiring in 1953. He moved to New York to continue work on his major project *The Negro in American Culture* (published posthumously). He died on 9 June 1954 in New York from heart complications.

Alain Locke Hall at Howard University is dedicated and named in his honour. The Hall is the site for the administrative offices of the College of Arts and Sciences as well as classrooms, learning labs and offices for the departments of English, Classics and Modern Languages and Literature.

Portrait by Betsy Graves Reyneau

JAMES ARTHUR HARLEY, 1873-1943
Jesus College

Anthropologist, theologian and local politician

Harley was born in Antigua on 15 May 1873 to Henry James Harley and Eleanora Josephine Lake. It is thought that his father was a landlord, but little is known about his early life, except that he attended the Mico training college in Antigua, in 1891.

Harley had a truly remarkable academic career; he attended Howard Law School in Washington, DC in 1902, then Yale in 1903 before going to Harvard to read for a bachelor's degree with honours in Semitic languages in 1906. At Harvard he received the first class Boylston elocution prize of $60 and two essay prizes valued at $50 and $25. He then won the Matthews Scholarship of $300 per year for three years, so left America for Oxford.

Harley matriculated at Jesus College to research for a BLitt, but in fact he obtained a third class honours degree in theology in 1909. He was also a special student at Manchester College (theological), which he left after a year. At Oxford, Harley was a member of the Oxford University branch of the Church Social Union and of the Anthropological Society. He was one of the first three students to take the Diploma of Anthropology at the Pitt Rivers Museum. His research work submitted at the time of examination was on Japanese Shintoism and its rationale. Harley gave a collection to the Pitt Rivers Museum in 1909 - a small collection consisting mainly of flint scrapers from Wookey Hole caves in Wells, Somerset, England.

Ordained on 29 September 1909 into the 'Diaconate' by the Lord Bishop of Peterborough, Harley was sent to St. Botolph's parish church, Shepshed, Leicestershire as a curate. Harley remained there

Harley (right) at the Pitt Rivers Museum

16

University of Oxford

THIS DIPLOMA IS TO CERTIFY
That *James Arthur Harley*
of *Jesus College* has pursued at Oxford
an approved course of study in ANTHROPOLOGY, and on
June 16, 1909 satisfied the Examiners appointed by
the University to examine in ANTHROPOLOGY.

(Signed)

Vice-Chancellor

Professor of Anthropology

only six months as he had to resign because of 'inordinate jealousy' on the part of the Reverend William Hepworth and, he states, 'on the part of some local folk who hated to see the church crammed with the "scum" they perceived' when he preached.

He was married in Oxford, on 1 July 1910, to Miss Josephine Maritcha Lawson, the daughter of Jesse Lawson, an African-American Howard University-educated lawyer; her mother was Rosetta C. Lawson, an advocate of temperance and low-income housing. Her parents founded the Frelinghuysen University in Washington, DC in 1917, to provide education, religious training and social services for Black working-class adults.

Harley took another curacy, in Chislet, near Canterbury, but the history of jealousy repeated itself. However, the work he delivered at his next curacy in Deal was such that the Archbishop of Canterbury, Randall Davison, recommended him for one of the best curacies in England - that of Windsor parish church, next door to the royal palace. But Harley felt unable to take up the position due to finances: he estimated that it would cost $3,000 a year to live up to

the position at Windsor. The Archbishop recommended an alternative posting to St. Leonard's parish church in Deal. Here he painted the church with his own hands and collected enough money to have the church furnished and restored. However, for a third time Harley found history repeating itself.

Disillusioned, he left the Church to play his part in the First World War. He attended classes in munitions manufacturing, one at King's College London, the other at Goldsmiths College. Becoming a skilled toolmaker, he returned to Shepshed to work at the local Shepshed lace firm, which at that time was making shell cases.

Harley started a second phase of his remarkable career by entering local politics as an independent councillor. His election posters of 1934 pulled no punches: they gave a breakdown of how the council had spent taxpayers' rates

The ordained James Arthur Harley

the previous year. His campaign slogan stated: 'Vote for Harley, the man for Charley' (Charnwood). He was elected a member of Leicestershire County Council, where he remained for thirteen years. He was also the chief officer in his constituency for civil defence and air raid welfare officer.

Harley also started his own weekly newspaper, *The Charnwood Bulletin*, which at first was free, but later cost 1d. It was in this and in the council chamber that at one time or other he slated every councillor. He would declare, 'If I am wrong then sue me.' No one ever did!

Harley died on 12 May 1943 of a seizure; he is buried at the churchyard of St. James the Greater in the hamlet of Oaks, Charnwood Forest, Leicestershire. He is still affectionately remembered today in Shepshed as 'Old Harley', and has a street named in his honour.

FEMALE RHODES SCHOLARS

'The greatest evil in omitting or misrepresenting Black history, literature, and culture in elementary or secondary education is the unmistakable message it sends to the black child. The message is "your history, your culture, your language and your literature are insignificant. And so are you."' Susan Rice, *A History Deferred*, 1986

CARLA PETERMAN, 1968-PRESENT
Oriel and New College

The first African-American woman Energy Commissioner

Carla Peterman became the first African-American female from a Historically Black College or University to earn the prestigious honour of being a Rhodes Scholar. Peterman, from South Orange, New Jersey, attended Howard University, where she earned a BA in history and received minors in environmental science and biology. In 1999 she matriculated at Oriel College to read for an MSc in environmental change and management followed by an MBA from New College.

Peterman states: 'Going to Oxford was my first time in Europe and I loved the history and historical setting. It was exciting to be living down the street from the site where Robert Hook discovered the cell. I also enjoyed my courses. They both had a diverse set of students from around the globe, and fieldwork that afforded me opportunities to travel throughout the UK and abroad.'

Peterman became a stellar researcher at the University of California Energy Institute at Haas and the Lawrence Berkeley National Laboratory. She has co-authored a series of publications on cost and deployment trends in the US solar photovoltaic market.

Appointed to the California Energy Commission in January 2011 by Governor Jerry Brown, and confirmed by the state senate in January 2012, Peterman became the first African-American woman, and the second African-American, to be appointed to the Commission. 'Oxford and my training there in environmental management, energy and business prepared me well for my role as an energy commissioner. It was there that I began to develop the tools to analyze energy problems with both a scientific and economic lens.'

Peterman was the lead commissioner for renewables, transportation, natural gas infrastructure and the Integrated Energy Policy Report. 'Some of my highest priorities were: implementing California's 33% renewable portfolio, development of a renewable strategic plan, and funding alternative fuels, vehicles, and infrastructure.' Peterman, appointed by the Governor of California in 2013, is the first African-American female California public utilities commissioner.

Oriel College

DR. SUSAN RICE, 1964-PRESENT
New College

The first African-American woman United States Ambassador to the United Nations

Rice comes from a family with esteemed educational credentials, well respected among the Washington elite. Her father, Emmett, was a Cornell University economics professor and former governor of the Federal Reserve System, while her mother, Lois, is an education policy researcher and guest scholar at the Brookings Institution. Her maternal grandparents were from Jamaica.

Her mother said, 'The one thing that was always a little challenge to me, from the time Susan was a baby, was that you could see when she was reaching a plateau, and she would always look at you as if to say, "What challenge are you going to give me next?"'

Rice grew up in a socially conscious household. When she was ten her family took a trip on Trans World Airlines' maiden voyage to the Middle East. Rice's family often spoke of politics and foreign policy at the dinner table. Her mother's job also brought notable figures through the house, including Madeleine Albright, with whom Rice's mother served on a local school board. Albright would later become a pivotal figure in Rice's personal and professional life.

Rice attended the National Cathedral School, a preparatory academy in Washington, DC. A gifted academic and athlete, she excelled in her academic courses, becoming her class valedictorian and illustrating her early political aptitude as president of the student council. Rice competed in three different sports, earning her the nickname 'Spo' (short for 'sportin') and went on to become a star point guard on the basketball team.

'She always excelled in school and developed an early interest in politics and public policy,' Rice's mother said of her daughter. 'It helped that she grew up in the nation's capital, where she went to school with children of congressmen and diplomats.' She also worked as a page, intern and research assistant in the US House of Representatives during high school and college.

Rice went to Stanford University in Palo Alto, California, where, pushing herself to excel, she earned Departmental Honours, University Distinction and became a Harry S. Truman scholar in 1984. This was a highly competitive and prestigious scholarship awarded to students with outstanding leadership potential and the ability to demonstrate a commitment to public service.

Elected to Phi Beta Kappa she made an impression on the heads of top

23

administrators by creating a fund that withheld alumni donations until the university either stopped their investments in companies doing business in South Africa, or the country ended apartheid.

After she received her bachelor's degree in history in 1986, Rice went on as a Rhodes Scholar to attend New College, Oxford, where she earned her MPhil and DPhil in international relations. Her dissertation examined Rhodesia's transition from white rule. Her paper won the Royal Commonwealth Society's Walter Frewen Lord prize for outstanding research in the field of Commonwealth history, as well as the Chatham House British International Studies Association prize for the most distinguished doctoral dissertation in the United Kingdom in the field of international relations.

She finished her academic schooling in 1990, and started work as an international management consultant at McKinsey & Company in Toronto, Canada. Between 1993 and 1995 Rice began work as the director of international organisation and peacekeeping for the National Security Council, where she had what she calls her 'most searing experience' when she visited Rwanda during a period in its history that was later classified as genocide.

Taking the lessons learned from her peacekeeping position to a new post as special assistant to President Clinton and senior director for African affairs, Rice became Assistant Secretary of State for African Affairs from 1997 to 2001. In recognition for her work and for distinguished contributions to the formation of

peaceful, cooperative relationships between states Rice was co-recipient of the White House's 2000 Samuel Nelson Drew memorial award.

In 2008 she became foreign policy adviser on Barack Obama's presidential campaign and a member of his presidential transition team, after his successful election in November of that year.

Nominated to be United States Ambassador to the United Nations, on 22 January 2009, confirmed by the United States Senate, Rice became the second youngest and the first African-American woman to be United States Ambassador to the United Nations.

KAREN LESLIE STEVENSON, 1956-PRESENT
Magdalen College

Attorney at Law and a double pioneer - the first African-American woman Rhodes Scholar and part of the first intake of women at Magdalen College

Born on 3 December 1956 in Beaumont, Texas, Stevenson grew up in Washington, DC where she was raised by a single mother and attended local public schools until eighth grade. Stevenson states that 'she had a thirst for knowledge and just enjoyed reading books and soaking up the information like a sponge'.

She attended the Taft School, a prestigious New England college preparatory school in Watertown, Connecticut. In 1975 Stevenson was awarded a Morehead Scholarship for leadership and academic excellence to attend the University of North Carolina at Chapel Hill receiving her BA in history in 1979, graduating Phi Beta Kappa. She was also a Jim Tatum scholar/athlete award winner and was inducted into the Order of the Golden Fleece leadership honour society. During her senior year she served as captain of the women's varsity track and field team.

Stevenson has the distinction of being the first African-American woman Rhodes Scholar, in 1979. She attended Magdalen College, where she earned her MA in modern European history. Of her Oxford experience, she recalls:

> Being the first African-American woman to receive the Rhodes generated a number of media events and interviews in America. When I arrived here it was not an issue or the focus of my experience. For me, arriving at the college and being among the first group of women admitted to the college, that was a much bigger challenge.
>
> To find a way to be myself and fit into this previously all male environment, the way that I dealt with being one of these new women was that I rowed for Worcester College. Magdalen did not yet have enough women to field a team, so that rowing experience really gave me a sense of belonging, community and fit with another group of smart athletic woman that was very important to me that year.

In 1980 her team succeeded in achieving four bumps during Torpids, the inter-collegiate rowing races. Stevenson still proudly displays her oar in her Los Angeles, California home.

Stevenson went on to earn a joint degree with distinction at Stanford Law

School. While there, with her teammate, Stevenson won the Marian Rice Kirkwood Moot Court award for Best Team of Advocates.

Recognition of her legal talents was highlighted three times, in 2005, 2007 and 2008 when she was selected a Southern California Super Lawyer Rising Star. She was also nominated by the Women Lawyers Association of Los Angeles as one of the Top 100 Women Litigators in Los Angeles. A skilled trial lawyer, Stevenson specializes in complex high stakes business litigation and trials for clients around the United States.

PRIME MINISTERS AND PRESIDENTS

'The medieval verdict of trial by water seemed child's play compared with the trial by dinner at All Souls.' Eric Williams

ERIC WILLIAMS, 1911-81
St. Catherine's Society
Trinidad and Tobago's first Prime Minister

The eldest of twelve children, Eric Eustace Williams, was born in Port of Spain, Trinidad and Tobago, on 25 September 1911. His mother, Elisa, was a housewife and his father, Henry, a junior civil servant in the post office.

Williams attend Queen's Royal College in Port of Spain and won an Island Scholarship. The director of the Education Department of Trinidad wrote to the master of University College, Oxford to commend Williams for a place at the College: 'Mr Williams,' he wrote, 'is not of European descent, but is a coloured boy, though not black. He comes of a good family and bears an excellent reputation as to his character and conduct in this colony. He is about average as an association footballer and is quite a good cricketer. I think you would find him acceptable as a member of your college.'

This testimonial was passed to the St. Catherine's Society (the forerunner of St. Catherine's College), where he became a non-collegiate student. Williams arrived at Oxford in 1932 to read history, much to the disappointment of his father, who wanted him to study either medicine or law. He was inspired intellectually, as he wrote later in the autobiographical *Inward Hunger:*

> The history and literature I had studied in Trinidad assumed new meaning at Oxford. Gladstone and Peel took on a new form - double firsts at Christ Church. My studies of the French Revolution and England after Waterloo received a new slant as I trod the colleges which had sheltered as undergraduates Charles James Fox and Canning, Salisbury and Rosebery, Cecil Rhodes and Lord Birkenhead. I retraced my private study of British Colonial history from 1700 to 1763 with the ghosts of William Penn, who had been expelled from Christ Church, Oglethorpe, who left Corpus Christi to found Georgia, George Whitfield who stalked Pembroke, Christopher Codrington, who endowed Codrington Library in All Souls, Chatham and North who, after leaving Trinity, were, the former to win America for Britain and the latter to lose most of it. Addison, Dr Samuel Johnson, Swift, Collins and Shelley, all came to life in Oxford. I heard not only the clash of arms and the battles of the books but also the throb of the Reformation.

He was awarded a first class degree, being placed - with two other students - first in the class. 'I had come, seen and conquered at Oxford - what next? My tutor and college principal was enormously pleased and vastly impressed; it was the first college First in history over a long period of years and we were agreed that to proceed to a diploma in education for a secondary school career in Trinidad was a sheer waste of time.'

The principal gave him a testimonial which read as follows: 'Mr E. E. Williams, who came to Oxford with a Trinidad government scholarship in 1932, has just crowned a successful career there by getting a brilliant First Class in Modern History. The competition in that examination is very severe but I have been told by one of the examiners that he was one of the best three men... The examiners openly congratulated him on his work.'

Williams returned to Oxford in the autumn of 1933 to follow his tutor's advice to read for a second honours in Philosophy, Politics and Economics (PPE) and to have a try at the All Souls Fellowship examination. Williams believed that racial prejudice impeded his success in obtaining the All Souls Fellowship, in which he came ninth out of sixteen candidates in the written examinations. The All Souls Fellowship 'immediately raised in my mind the question of racial prejudice. I asked both [the principal and his tutor] very frankly what they thought. My tutor pooh-poohed the idea; the principal advised me that, if I were after a "social" fellowship, one involving principally tutoring, my race would be against me, but that I would be eligible for a fellowship based on merit.'

Williams completed his thesis, 'The Economic Aspects of the Abolition of the West Indian Slave Trade and Slavery', in which he argued that the commercial capitalism of the eighteenth century developed the wealth of Europe by means of slavery and monopoly and that British economic self-interest rather than humanitarianism constituted the motive force for the emancipation

Bachelor's Degree: Oxford 1935

of the slaves. Williams was awarded a DPhil in 1938. 'My research degree immediately faced me with the problem of a job. England was clearly out of the question; there were too many senior people at Oxford, including the Dean of my college who was so impressed with my Latin background, who, on seeing me would say: "Are you still here? You had better go back home. You West Indians are too keen on trying to get posts here which take jobs away from Englishmen." There was no misunderstanding such frankness.'

In 1939 Williams accepted a post at Howard University, which he dubbed 'Negro Oxford', as assistant Professor of Social and Political Science. 'The novelty - for me - of a University comprising different faculties as against constituent, virtually autonomous colleges, defined the visible differences between White Oxford in England on the banks of the Isis and "Negro Oxford" in America suitably far, in a Jim Crow milieu, from the banks of the Potomac.'

In 1944 Williams was appointed to the Anglo-American Caribbean Commission, a body formed to analyze and recommend measures to improve the common social and economic problems of the region, and its successor, the Caribbean Commission.

His thesis formed the seminal book *Capitalism and Slavery*, which was also published in 1944, when Williams was thirty-three. The book, which reinforced the so-called 'Williams thesis' that slavery fuelled early capitalism and was abolished through the profit motive rather than humanitarianism, was applauded in some quarters and received severe criticism in others. In 1948 he returned to Trinidad where, after some years in research and academic work, he turned to full-time politics, forming the People's National Movement (PNM) in 1956. His speeches delivered to crowds in Port of Spain's Woodford Square earned him a large popular following, and his criticism of British colonialism in the run-up to independence in 1962, struck a chord with Trinidad and Tobago's electorate. In one speech delivered in June 1955, he told his audience:

I was born here, and here I stay, with the people of

Surrounded by youth of the nation

Trinidad & Tobago, who educated me free of charge for nine years at Queen's Royal College and for five years at Oxford, who have made me whatever I am, and who have been or might be at any time the victims of the very pressure which I have been fighting against for 12 years… I am going to let down my bucket where I am, right here with you in the British West Indies.

He was elected in 1956 and became Chief Minister in the country's first self-rule government from 1956 to 1959. In December 1961 he won a landslide victory to become the independent nation's first Prime Minister, a position he held - despite economic problems and political dissent - until his death.

A noted historian, Williams wrote extensively on Caribbean politics and history, his books include: *British Historians and the West Indies; From Columbus to Castro: The History of the Caribbean 1492-1969; Inward Hunger: The Education of a Prime Minister; Education in the British West Indies; The Negro in the Caribbean; History of the People of Trinidad and Tobago; and Documents of West Indian History.*

Recognized as one of the most significant leaders in the history of modern Trinidad and Tobago, Williams is often referred to as the 'Father of the Nation'.

He was made an Honorary Fellow of St. Catherine's during his visit to witness the official opening of the College on 16 October 1964. In the same year he was made a member of Her Majesty's Privy Council and in 1965 he was awarded an honorary DCL by the University. He was made a Companion of Honour in 1969.

Eric Williams in discussion with Winston Churchill

SIR GRANTLEY ADAMS, 1898-1971
St. Catherine's Society

Barbados' first Premier and Prime Minister of the West Indies Federation

Grantley Herbert Adams, the third of Fitzherbert Adams and Rosa Frances Turney's seven children, was born on 28 April 1898 in a modest little cottage called Colliston, on Government Hill in Barbados. His father was the head teacher of one of the island's largest primary school, St. Giles, and this is where the young Adams started his education. He was tutored by his father to win a scholarship to the prestigious Harrison College. A bright student, Adams won the Barbados Scholarship in 1918, yet stayed in Barbados for a year as a staff member of Harrison College.

The Barbados Scholarship enabled him to attend St. Catherine's Society to study law and classics. The Scholarship provided a modest allowance of £175 - later raised to £250 per year.

Arriving at Oxford in September 1919, Adams, as a non-collegiate student, had to live in student digs in Bartlemas Road, off Cowley Road. Throughout his time at Oxford Adams played cricket, a passion and love which he derived from his father. In one memorable match against Hertford College he had the satisfaction of scoring four sixes in one over. He became secretary of the Justinian Law Society, and was elected to a Librarian Exhibition at St. Catherine's, valued at £30 a year. He joined the St. Catherine's Debating Society, of which he was to become president; he was also elected president of St. Catherine's Society's Junior Common Room.

While in Oxford Adams met and became friends with a number of other Barbadians and West Indian students who shared his passion for cricket. Noel 'Crab' Nethersole, a student at Lincoln College, described as a demon left hand bowler and a genius for public finance, combined his love for both when he later became Jamaica's Minister of Finance and the Jamaican representative on the West Indian Cricket Board of Control. He also became a prominent member of the People's National Party and a chief adviser to Norman Manley (see p.38). Another contemporary was Sidney Van Sertima, the British Guiana Scholar in 1916. He achieved a First in British Civil Law, won the Barstow Scholarship and was runner-up for an All Souls Fellowship. Returning to Guiana he established himself as one of the leading barristers in the country and the West Indies.

During the 1922 Easter holidays Adams worked at his legal studies in Hastings with a Barbadian friend, H. A. M. Beckles. Beckles studied French at Oxford, won the Heath Harrison Scholarship in French and lived in Paris for two years. He later became deputy principal of Queen's College, British Guiana.

Adams also met Erskine Ward, another Barbadian, who became Speaker of the West Indies Federation House of Representatives. During the summer vacation of 1922 Adams and Ward cycled from Oxford to Torquay for a holiday with Lionel Reeves, another Barbadian. They played cricket for Torquay and cycled all over south Devon. Reeves read medicine at University College London and became a general practitioner in southern England.

As a result of specializing in Ecclesiastical Law and becoming interested in theology, Adams met the Barbadian principal of Wycliffe Hall, an evangelical theological college situated in Banbury Road, Oxford. The Reverend H. B. Gooding had been the Barbados Scholar of 1906 and won a first in classics and theology. The two became great friends, and every Sunday, Adams and Ward used to visit Gooding, attracted not only by the religious discussion but by the exquisite teas that were served to them. The Rev. Gooding, as Rector of St. John's Church, Barbados, would later preside over Adams' wedding to Grace Thorne in 1929.

Having heard the Liberal Leader H. H. Asquith in a debate with L. E. Wharton from Trinidad at the Oxford Union Society, Adams became an active member of the Liberal Party at Oxford - inspired by the party's achievements in social legislation. As a Liberal, Adams campaigned for Frank Gray, an Oxford solicitor who won the parliamentary seat for the City of Oxford in the 1923 by-election, and for C. B. Fry who unsuccessfully contested the seat the following year.

Adams left Oxford in 1923 and was called to the Bar at Gray's Inn. He returned to Barbados in 1925 and became the leading Labour politician there. His legal training and intellect made him an articulate opponent of the conservative colonial establishment during the turbulent 1930s, a period of unrest that culminated in riots in 1937. After being elected to the House of Assembly in 1934, 1935 and 1936, he helped form the Barbados Labour Party (BLP) in 1938. Adams was soon elected leader of the BLP, a position which he held until 1941. Just two years after being launched, the BLP won five seats in the House of Assembly.

Adams and others established the Barbados Workers' Union (BWU) in October 1941 with a remit to empower the island's poor Black working class in various trades and occupations. Adams acted as President of the BWU until 1954, when he became the first Premier of Barbados as leader of the BLP. In the 1956 election the BLP won a majority of seats in the House and Adams was re-elected as Premier.

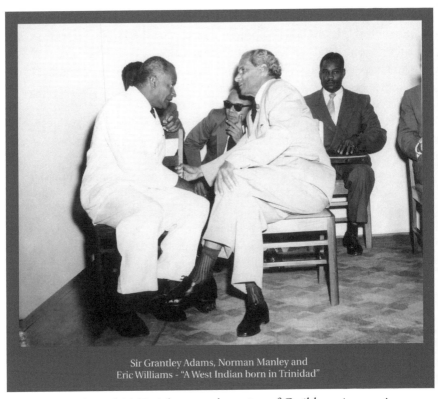

Sir Grantley Adams, Norman Manley and
Eric Williams - "A West Indian born in Trinidad"

Between 1958 and 1962, Adams - a champion of Caribbean integration – was Prime Minister of the short-lived West Indies Federation, a political grouping of British colonies in the region. When the Federation was disbanded he returned to political life in Barbados and was Leader of the Opposition from 1966 until his retirement in 1970.

Theodore Sealy in his *Sealy's Caribbean Leaders* described Adams as 'a figure challenging the past to build a new future'. Unquestionably, Adams was a powerful and influential leader in the social revolution of Barbados, specifically in dethroning the country's ruling 'plantocracy'. He is also credited with a great deal of social reform and changes to legislation such as improved working conditions for women, attainment of a full ministerial government, improved health facilities and minimum wage legislation. According to the Caribbean Community Secretariat:

> Barbados' current political stability and level of economic development has its underpinnings in the formidable foundation Adams managed to establish in his movement to secure social and economic development

and political reform in the Island State. His leadership produced a diversified Barbados economy. The Barbados Development Board was established. There was significant reform and rehabilitation in the social sector, particularly in education, health and housing. Modernisation of the education system, introduction of a Teachers' Training Programme in the form of the Ediston Teachers' College in 1948, the construction of new housing schemes and roads are some of the hallmarks of his achievements as a political leader. Symbols of the high honour he was accorded still exist today in the nation he so loved. Barbados' international airport bears his name, the Grantley Adams International Airport, and his image appears on the highest currency note, the $100 bill.

Adams was made a Companion in the Most Distinguished Order of St. Michael and St. George in the New Year's Honours List of 1952 and knighted in 1957 by Her Majesty, The Queen of England. One of Barbados' ten National Heroes, a statute of Adams is erected at the entrance to Government Headquarters in Bridgetown, the country's capital. Sir Grantley Adams died at the age of 73 of a cerebral haemorrhage on 28 November 1971.

TOM ADAMS, 1931-85
Magdalen College

Barbados' second Prime Minister

Know by many as a man with a handsome presence, a gift of persuasive eloquence and an outstanding personality, Jon Michael Geoffrey Manningham Adams became Barbados' second Prime Minister. Born on 24 September 1931, an only child, his impressive list of names was a result of his parents' admiration and gratitude for various people.

His father, Grantley Adams, admired the British advocate Sir John Simons and wanted him called John; however, this was misspelt on his birth certificate as Jon. His mother, Grace, liked the name Michael and thought that Geoffrey was also pleasant. In wanting to express her gratitude to the doctor, Gerald Manningham, who saved her and her son's life after a difficult birth, she added Manningham to his name. Although Tom was not added to the names he was christened with, he is always referred to as 'Tom' Adams.

Tom was a sickly child. Born as a 'blue baby', he had bouts of ill health throughout his childhood, which at one point led the Adams to secure a home tutor. Like his father, Tom entered Bridgetown's Harrison College, where he demonstrated an impressive intellect and a gift for oratory. He was also the editor of a mathematics magazine, the *Mathematics Announcer*.

He was *Proxime Accessit,* (runner up) in the Barbados Scholarship in 1949; he also won the Hawkins Memorial Prize. In the following year he achieved the Barbados Scholarship in the study of mathematics.

Tom entered Oxford (unlike his father, a non-collegiate student) as a member

Magdalen College, New Building

of Magdalen College to read Philosophy, Politics and Economics (PPE). After spending a year in residence at Magdalen, he moved to digs at 5 Pusey Street.

At Oxford he continued his friendships with Fabian Holder, the Barbados Scholar of 1948, who was at Oriel College. School friends in the fifth and sixth form at Harrison College, they also produced the college magazine. His circle of friends also included Hector Wynter, Emile George, Asquith Philips, George Moe, Denys and Colin Williams and Eddie Braithwaite.

Tom played an active part in the politics of West Indian students, becoming a member of the Oxford branch of the Labour Party. He canvassed for the Labour Party at election time and was active during the party conference in Blackpool. In 1952 he served as an unofficial personal assistant to Hugh Gaitskell.

He gained his BA in November 1954, proceeding to the MA degree in July 1958.

After leaving Oxford, Tom worked for the British Broadcasting Corporation (BBC) as a freelance writer and producer for a daily World Service programme *Caribbean Voices*. He also met his wife, Genevieve Turner, a secretary, whilst at the BBC in 1957.

Politics continue to attract him in London and he associated with leading members of the British Labour Party, including his Oxford contemporary Shirley Williams, later a founder and prominent member of the Social Democratic Party. Following in his father's footsteps, he enrolled as a student of Gray's Inn, and was called to the Bar in 1965. Tom returned to Barbados and his childhood home, Tyrol Cot, in 1963, and was elected to the newly independent parliament in 1966, becoming the official Leader of the Opposition five years later.

Tom became Prime Minister in 1976 after leading the Barbados Labour Party to victory against the Democratic Labour Party that year. He replaced Errol Barrow, Barbados' first Prime Minister, who had been in office from 1966. His party won again in 1981. He was expected to win a third election before his sudden death in 1985, when he collapsed of a heart attack, aged 53. Tom's term of office lasted from 8 September 1976 until 11 March 1985.

Tom Adams is remembered as an articulate and forceful politician, at times controversial and even abrasive. His decision to support the US-led invasion of Grenada after the murder of Maurice Bishop was much criticized in Barbados and beyond, but, according to Dean Harold Crichlow, who delivered the eulogy at his funeral, 'he had the courage to face world criticism in support of a cause which he believed threatened world peace.'

NORMAN MANLEY, 1893-1969
Jesus College

Barrister and Jamaica's first Premier

Norman Washington Manley was born near Porus, in the parish of Manchester, Jamaica, on 4 July 1893. His father, Albert Manley, was a produce dealer, the son of a Jamaican woman and a Yorkshireman; his mother was almost 'pure white'. Manley recalled that he grew up as a 'bush man', earning pocket money for clearing pastures, chipping logwood and herding cattle.

He attended Jamaica College on a half scholarship from 1906 to 1913. He was a difficult student there, better known for his troublemaking than for his academic record. His mother, however, wished for him to go to Oxford, so encouraged him to apply for a Rhodes Scholarship, in which he was successful.

Arriving in England just before the outbreak of the First World War, he was admitted to Jesus College as a Rhodes Scholar. The University was unusually quiet, as many young men had left to fight in Europe. In 1915 he enlisted in the army with his brother Roy, as a private in the Royal Field Artillery, refusing to be made an officer; instead fighting with the rank and file of 'cockneys with a view of life all their own'. Three years of active service on the Western Front, including the battles of the Somme and Ypres, brought him both sorrow and glory. His brother Roy was killed in action in 1917, and Manley was decorated with a Military Medal for bravery in action.

Resuming his studies at Oxford in 1919, he was an outstanding athlete and scholar. A report of the March 1921 inter-collegiate athletics competition remarked: 'Most of our representatives did well, particularly D. Davis and NW Manley. How the college would have fared without them in the early stages of the cup is not a very comfortable thought.'

The March 1920 journal of the literary Neo Hellenist Society reported that 'Mr Manley

Manley the scholar

made an excellent contribution to the discussion of Bernard Shaw's *The Doctor's Dilemma,* in a study of the play from a literary and satiric standpoint'. The Society's 'members met for the 3rd meeting of term to hear Mr Manley read a paper on "Samuel Butler" which proved to be one of the cleverest contributions that have been made to the transactions of the society. Mr Manley evidently knew his subject thoroughly and he expressed his conclusions in a style as brilliant and with critical insight as penetrating as any we have been privileged to hear at meetings of the society.' Manley graduated with a degree in jurisprudence in 1921, gaining not only second class honours, but also the certificate of honour in the Bar finals.

In the same year he married his cousin, Edna Swithenbank, an artist and sculptress; they later had two sons, Douglas and Michael. He spent some time in the Chambers of S. C. N. Goodman, following a number of advocates all over court, and learning not only technique but style.

Manley returned to Jamaica in August 1922. On the boat journey he had a chance meeting with Sir John Simon, the renowned English advocate, who was on his way to holiday in Jamaica. According to Manley, this man taught him through their informal discussions 'more about the art of advocacy in ten days than I had learnt in all my life'.

Manley became a successful barrister in Kingston, with a number of exciting cases catching the public attention: the Spalding murder trial of 1924, the Walker trial of 1927 and the Alexander trial of 1931. He gained a reputation, which serves as a guide to all aspiring advocates to this day, for painstaking and meticulous research and analysis of every aspect of his case. Manley appeared in every important case, civil and criminal, in Jamaica between 1923 and 1955.

In 1938 he supported the Banana Producers' Association in their labour conflict and acted as their barrister. Amidst mounting social tension he co-founded with his cousin, the future Prime Minister Alexander Bustamante, the People's National Party (PNP) that same year. Committed to social reform and universal suffrage, the PNP was instrumental in the struggle for Jamaican independence. Manley served as Jamaica's first Chief Minister from 1955 to 1959, becoming Jamaica's first Premier from 1959 to 1962. Manley played a key role in the practical implementation of independence for Jamaica, leading the team of negotiators who worked with the British. He was also a leading advocate of the Federation of the West Indies, a political formation opposed by Bustamante, who had split from the PNP and founded the Jamaica Labour Party in 1943. Manley spent much of his political career in the shadow of his more populist cousin but was widely respected as a champion of social justice.

In his last speech to a PNP annual conference, he remarked:

Norman Manley at a conference, 1960

I say that the mission of my generation was to win self-government for Jamaica. To win political power which is the final power for the black masses of my country from which I spring. I am proud to stand here today and say to you who fought that fight with me, say it with gladness and pride: Mission accomplished for my generation… And what is the mission of this generation?… It is… reconstructing the social and economic society and life of Jamaica.

Spending his last years as Leader of the Opposition, shortly before his death he was proclaimed a National Hero of Jamaica. Manley died in September 1969 at the age of seventy-two. Edna Manley sent a hand written response to the letter written to her by the college on his death:

11th October 1969

Thank you for your letter on behalf of the college where my husband spent a period of his life that helped shape his destiny. He always spoke of Oxford with great affection & a lovely photo of Jesus College still hangs in his room.

I miss him terribly, & I think the West Indies have felt the loss very deeply.

Two portraits of Manley can be found in Oxford: one at Rhodes House and the other in the dining hall of Jesus College.

SIR SERETSE KHAMA, 1921-80
Balliol College

Botswana's first Prime Minister and the country's first President

Khama was born in Serowe, in the British Protectorate of Bechuanaland, on 1 July 1921. His grandfather, Kgama III, was paramount chief (*Kgosi*) of the Bama-Ngwato, who formed part of the Tswana people of the region. At the age of four, after the death of Kgama III, Seretse Khama to all extents and purposes became *Kgosi*.

He was educated in South Africa and graduated with a BA from Fort Hare College in 1944. The following year Khama left for England, matriculating at Balliol College to study law, followed by further studies at the Inner Temple, London. His first experiences at Oxford were not positive: 'I was miserable for the first term,' he later recalled, 'I thought I was intensely disliked because nobody talked to me or showed any interest in me and I thought it was just another way of showing me that I did not belong.' The second term was better, however, as Khama made friends and played rugby for Balliol. A booklet entitled *A Background Study of the Southern African Crisis* would later be published by the Oxford University Socialist Club, authored by Khama. He did not take his exams at Oxford as it was discovered that he lacked the necessary competence in Latin.

In June 1947 Khama first met Ruth Williams, a WAAF ambulance driver during the Second World War, now working as a clerk at Lloyds. Their marriage in September 1948 caused considerable political controversy in southern Africa.

The marriage of a Black chief to a British white woman was problematic, as the prevailing Apartheid government had banned interracial marriages in South Africa. His uncle attempted to disrupt the marriage, demanding that Khama return home to have it annulled. Interrupting his law studies, Khama returned home with the momentous task ahead of him of persuading the Bama-Ngwato people of his continued suitability as chief. On 21 June 1949 at a *Kgotla*, a meeting of the elders, he was pronounced *Kgosi*, and his new wife was made welcome.

Returning to Britain to continue his law studies, he was still plagued with problems; the British government, which controlled Bechuanaland, demanded a parliamentary investigation into his suitability for the chieftaincy. Khama and his wife were banished from Bechuanaland in 1950 for six years.

Britain relented and allowed the couple to return to Bechuanaland, but only if Khama and his uncle accepted the condition of renouncing their claim to the chieftaincy. In presenting this deal, the British government underestimated Kama's political currency back home as a result of his six years in exile.

In 1962 Khama founded the Bechuanaland Democratic Party and at its head began a campaign for social and multi-racial reform. His main objective, however, was independence. In 1965 the Bechuanaland government was moved from Mafeking in South Africa to the newly established capital of Gaborone - and Khama was elected as Prime Minister. When the country achieved independence on 30 September 1966, Khama became the first president of the Republic of Botswana. He was re-elected twice. In 1966 Elizabeth II appointed Khama Knight Commander of the Most Excellent Order of the British Empire.

Khama used his considerable influence among the country's various ethnic groups and traditional chiefs to create a strong, democratic government. During his rule Botswana had the fastest growing economy of the world, and the discovery of diamond deposits allowed the government to finance the creation of a new social infrastructure. He also played an important role in the shift from white minority rule in Rhodesia to the creation of a democratic Zimbabwe. On 13 July 1980 Khama died in office of pancreatic cancer.

A MARRIAGE OF INCONVENIENCE

THE PERSECUTION OF SERETSE & RUTH KHAMA

MICHAEL DUTFIELD

NOW A MAIOR T.V. DOCUMENTARY

KOFI ABREFA BUSIA, 1913-78
University College

Academic and Prime Minister of Ghana

Born in Wenchi in the Ashanti Confederacy (one of the four British-controlled Gold Coast territories – now Ghana) on 11 July 1913, Busia was the eldest of thirteen children. He was raised by the Methodist missionaries, Rev. William Whittle and his wife Alice, who arrived in Wenchi when he was about ten. His father sent the young Busia to these missionaries, and in exchange for a European education, he became their steward boy.

At the end of the nineteenth century the Methodists had established what remains today one of the most distinguished private boarding schools on the Cape Coast, Mfantsipim College, and there were exams for scholarships. Rev. Whittle, realizing Busia's academic brilliance, encouraged him to go to Kumasi to sit the exam for the Methodist Synod scholarship; he came top in the country.

Once at Mfantsipim College, Busia excelled in his studies. At home with his mother, he vowed three things: to build a house in his beloved Wenchi, to go to Oxford University - which he had heard so much about from the Rev. Whittle - and to make his country a better place, not just for the fortunate, but for the poor and disenfranchised.

On completing his schooling at Mfantsipim, Busia then attended teacher training at Wesley College, Kumasi, in 1931, and taught as a student/teacher at Achimota School in 1935. Busia was then selected for an Achimota Council Scholarship, and after sitting for an external BA honours degree in medieval and modern history from London University, he received another Achimota Scholarship to go and study at Oxford.

Busia constantly challenged cultural notions about adopting and adapting of all things British as appropriate and proper. Throughout his schooling his teachers insisted on calling him George Frederick. His father had named him Kofi Abrefa, and he legally changed his name back before going to Oxford.

Busia travelled to England to study for his BA in Politics, Philosophy and Economics (PPE) at University College, Oxford, where he was the first matriculated African student. His daughter, Abena, recalls two incidents her father told her about when he first arrived at Oxford.

For British colonial schoolchildren, Empire Day (24 May, Queen Victoria's birthday) had been the biggest and most important day in the school year, a major holiday with no school. Instead pupils all had to learn to sing 'patriotic' songs and would get dressed up for a big parade. In Busia's first year as an undergraduate at Oxford, he got up and got dressed, eagerly expecting that grand as such parades were in Ghana, they would be even more special in England itself. He asked where the parade would pass in Oxford. Everybody looked at him in bewilderment because nobody knew what he was talking about. That was when he realized one of the most effective tools of empire was propaganda. Empire Day was only celebrated in the far flung parts of the empire and it was not celebrated in Britain itself; it was a big lesson to him. People who were born and brought up in Britain had never heard of Empire Day.

The second story concerned the idea of formal dress. When Busia arrived at Oxford, for formal dinners in the evening students wore appropriate formal dress, as well as gowns. If they did not show up suitably dressed, they would be 'sconced', which meant they would be forced to drink a tankard of beer in one, and if they refused or failed would have to deliver a defence of themselves in Latin. Abena recalls:

> My father wanted to make a point about the definition and interpretation of appropriate attire. As far as he was concerned, our wonderful Kente cloth was very formal. The craft takes years to learn and the finished cloth can cost hundreds of pounds; it is the cloth of kings. My father felt that the narrow interpretation of formal dress as tails and bow tie was inappropriate. As a Latin and classics scholar he did indeed prepare a speech, in Latin - on the meaning of civilization and in the defence of his dress. He came on a Thursday night in Kente cloth, the finest of our formal traditions. The whole dining hall started shouting, 'Sconce him! Sconce him! Sconce him!'
>
> His friends were nervous because they knew he was a teetotaller, but my father wanted to deliver his defence of Ghanaian dress in Latin. Unfortunately for him, the hall master looked at him and said, 'Oh leave him alone, he's just homesick!' And so he never got to deliver his speech.

After studying for two years, instead of three, Busia received his BA degree in 1941. A young Harold Wilson, who later became British Prime Minister, was one of his economics tutors. He received his MA in 1946 and his DPhil in Social Anthropology in 1947 with a thesis entitled "The position of the chief in the modern political system of Ashanti: a study of the influence of contemporary social changes on Ashanti political institutions". He married in Oxford at the Wesley Memorial Church on 14 August 1950, his wedding to Naa-Morkor, a Ghanaian midwife and teacher, making the *Oxford Times* newspaper under the headline 'All African Wedding at Oxford'.

Busia achieved a number of firsts in his distinguished career. He became the first of two Africans appointed to the British Colonial Service as district commissioner, the first African professor at the University College of the Gold Coast, Ghana and by royal appointment the first African to hold a professorship at the University of Leiden in Holland since Johannes Capitein in the eighteenth century; he was also a Professor of Sociology and a Senior Member of St. Antony's College, Oxford, from 1962 to 1969.

'All-African' Wedding at Oxford

The bride and bridegroom, with a group of those who took part in the ceremony.

AN "all-African" wedding was recently solemnised at the Wesley Memorial Methodist Church, Oxford. African dress was worn by the bride (Miss Victoria Naa-Morkor Bruce), the bridegroom (Dr. Kofi A. Busia), the best man (Mr. Buatin K. Busia), the bride's cousin (Mr. E. A. Quist-Areton), who gave her away, and the chief bridesmaid (Miss Adeline Leigh), all from the Gold Coast. The groomsmen and several guests were similarly attired, providing a bright and colourful setting for a most moving and significant ceremony.

The bridegroom, Dr. Busia, at present on the staff of the University College of the Gold Coast, is a graduate of University College and in 1941 secured his B.A. degree, and in 1947 his thesis gained for him his doctorate of philosophy. He has just returned from a visit to the United States, where he has been in close con-

sultation with the heads of the social science sections of several universities there. The bride (Miss Bruce) is a fully trained nurse and midwife from Accra, and has had some experience in the Churchill Hospital, Oxford.

The wedding was conducted by two former Gold Coast missionaries, the Rev. William Whittle, in whose home Dr. Busia lived during his early years, and the Rev. Maurice H. Giddings, who exercised a great influence upon his life at a later stage. The Rev. W. Bardsley Brash also took part in the service.

There were two additional bridesmaids, Miss Natalie Fortes, the daughter of Dr. and Mrs. M. Fortes, of Oxford, and Miss Rachel Giddings, younger daughter of the Rev. and Mrs. M. H. Giddings, of Brigg. Dr. D. Parker was at the organ. The reception was held in the church hall. Dr. and Mrs. Busia are now on their way to the Gold Coast.

Aside from his formidable academic achievements, Busia was drawn to politics and, in particular, to opposition to Kwame Nkrumah, the dominant and radical political figure who led Ghana to independence in 1957. His anti-Nkrumah activity meant that Busia felt his life was threatened, and his years in Leiden and Oxford were essentially periods of exile. In 1966 he returned to Ghana after Nkrumah's overthrow by the military and he later formed the Progress Party, successor to the United Party, which had been in opposition to Nkrumah at the time of independence. In 1969 his party won the election, gaining 105 of the 140 constituencies - a record unbeaten to this day. Busia served as Prime Minister from October 1968 to January 1972, when another military coup took place while he was having a medical check-up in Britain. His political record was mixed; he presided over unpopular austerity policies and a major devaluation, which caused widespread social unrest.

Busia is regarded as one of Africa's most influential scholars, whose parallel academic and political careers were shaped by an abiding and consistent concern for the people of Africa and the principles of democratic rule. He died in 1978 in exile in Oxford, and his body was later returned to Ghana for a state funeral in Accra and burial in Wenchi.

LEGAL EAGLES

'I am the Zulu who graduated from Columbia last spring. I am studying law here. Oxford is full of inspiration. Your older son ought to be here.' Pixley Ka Isaka Seme, letter to Booker T. Washington, 29 January 1907

EDWARD T. NELSON, 1874-1940
St. John's College

Barrister and local politician

Edward Theophilus Nelson, the son of Philip Nelson, a British Guiana builder, was born on 22 October 1874 in Georgetown, the colony's capital. He attended the prestigious Queen's College in Georgetown, where he gained a place at Oxford to read law at St. John's College in 1898. In the last term of his second year he was elected secretary of the Oxford Union, working with its president, Prime Minister Asquith's son Raymond; he became treasurer by the beginning of his third year.

The news reached Nelson's homeland, and Georgetown's *Argosy* newspaper of 31 March 1900 noted that a Black self-help agricultural society had cabled congratulations to Edward Nelson; the appointment to be treasurer was also noted in the newspaper on 21 July 1990.

Nelson at St. John's (back row, left)

In 1902 Nelson graduated with a third class degree, and moved to London where he was called to the Bar at Lincoln's Inn on 17 November 1904. Nelson was one of the first West Indians, if not the first, to be allowed to wear the stuff gown, a gown worn by a barrister who is not a Queen's (or King's) Counsel in the English Courts.

In 1906 he moved to Bowdon in Cheshire and opened a legal practice at 78 King Street, Manchester. He married and had a daughter, living the life of a middle-class professional gentleman.

In 1909 The Gorse Hall Murder took place, an infamous case involving the murder of landowner George Harry Storrs at his home Gorse Hall in Stalybridge, Cheshire. Nelson came to prominence by successfully defending Mark Wilde, the Crown's accused. The *Liverpool Echo* concluded: 'He so ably defended Wilde.' Recognition of his ability came with the award of the Queen's Coronation medal. Nelson was also counsel in three cases involving legal points considered of sufficient significance to reach *The Law Reports:* R v Naguib (1916); R v Watson (1917); and Simcock v Simcock (1932).

Most of his working life was devoted to civic affairs and local politics. In March 1913 he stood as a Conservative for the west ward of Hale urban district council; his opponent, William H. Hughes, secured only 91 votes against Nelson's 224. The *Altrincham, Bowdon and Hale Guardian* noted: 'As a barrister, Mr Nelson has a good name, and the interest he has taken in local affairs was not one of the least of the credentials he presented. In Mr Hughes he had an opponent of some personal popularity and with some claim to public regard, and his success is naturally the source of a good deal of elation among his supporters, who feel that in Mr Nelson they have a representative who is well able to protect their interest.'

One other more public act took place in 1919, when he successfully defended African dockworkers accused of rioting in Liverpool. The *Liverpool Daily Post and Mercury* of 8 November 1919 reported under the headline 'The racial riots - Coloured Men on Trial at Liverpool Assizes':

> Fifteen coloured men were placed on trial for…the racial riots in the city in June last. Mr Nelson (who is a coloured gentleman) appeared for the prisoners. The events of early June had seen 700 coloured men and their families removed from their homes in the Pitt Street area of Liverpool, one Black drowned, and a policeman injured. Two Russians sailors gave evidence and Nelson told the court that '*there was strong antipathy on the part of Scandinavians and Russians against sailing with coloured men*'. The event was a major one for the Black community of Liverpool.

The newspaper on 10 November noted the comments of the court shorthand writer: 'I have never seen so many men of colour in a court of justice since I left Alabama 50 years ago.' He also observed that, as well as the 15 accused, there were 'an equal number of their native friends, together with a native barrister (who conducted the defence with great clearness and ability)'. Nelson's work on the 10 November led to one William Green being discharged.

Nelson became chairman of the Hale library committee at the beginning of 1921 and remained in that position until July 1939. In 1937 he became chairman of the Hale Council. His years of experience led to his appointment as chairman of the Cheshire Urban District Councils' Association. Nelson remained a member of Hale Council until his death on 3 August 1940, aged sixty-six.

PIXLEY KA ISAKA SEME, 1881-1951
Jesus College

Political activist, lawyer, journalist and founder of the African National Congress

The son of Isaka Seme and his wife Sarah (*née* Mseleku), Pixley Ka Isaka Seme was born on 2 October 1881 in Natal, South Africa. His parents died when he was young, and he was educated at the local primary mission school, where the American Congregationalist missionary, Rev. S. C. Pixley, took an interest in his development, arranging for him to attend Northfield Mount Hermon School in Massachusetts, America.

Seme continued his studies as an undergraduate at Columbia University in New York, where he received his Bachelor of Arts. He was the first Black South African to study there. With a memorable speech entitled 'The Regeneration of Africa' Seme received the George William Curtis medal, the university's highest oratorical honour.

Thanks to financial assistance from missionaries, he was admitted to Jesus College, Oxford in September 1906 to read law. His grandson, Vezindaba Seme, of Umlazi, later said that his grandfather received this financial backing because the missionaries recognized his 'vision and political assertiveness'.

At Oxford Seme went riding with Alain Locke (see p.13) and was a member of the Cosmopolitan Club. He also founded a club for African students. His interest in debate and current affairs led him to join the Oxford Union. According to the *Oxford Dictionary of National Biography*:

> At his lodgings in Beaumont Street, where he resumed his

The Cosmopolitan Club (Seme 3rd from left, Locke 3rd from right, back row)

friendship with the African-American Alain Locke (1886-1955), he hired a piano and took up pipe-smoking. He joined the Oxford Union and became treasurer of the Cosmopolitan Club for students from abroad. He ate dinners at the Middle Temple and from early 1908 spent more time in London than in Oxford, often listening to debates in the House of Commons. Not being able to find vacation work, he fell into financial difficulties from which he was not able to extricate himself until after his return to South Africa.

Seme became the first Zulu ever to graduate from the University when he gained a BA in Civil Law in June 1909. He passed his first Bar examinations, and the following year was called to the Bar at the Middle Temple, London. In 1910 back in South Africa Seme set up a large legal practice in Johannesburg, where his clients included the Swazi royal family.

He produced a seminal text entitled 'Native Union' in 1911, appearing in various newspapers. It called for the making of a modern African political organization and became the founding document for the South African Native National Congress. On 8 January 1912 Seme and several of his colleagues convened a convention that led to the creation of the South African Native

National Congress (SANNC), later renamed the African National Congress (ANC) in 1923. Seme suggested that the new organization should be modelled on the United States Congress. He became its treasurer general.

The Queen Regent of Swaziland provided Seme with the funds to launch the ANC newspaper *Abantu Batho*. The paper achieved nationwide circulation and was printed in Zulu, Xhosa, Sotho and English; it continued publication for over twenty years. Seme's record with the newspaper was mixed and he ran it through a turbulent period. In 1930 he became the ANC's president-general, but his tenure was marked by divisions and political confusion.

In 1928 his prestige was further enhanced when Columbia University, his alma mater, awarded him an Honorary Doctorate of Law (LLD). Seme married the daughter of Dinizulu, paramount chief of the Zulus. They had four sons and one daughter. He died in Johannesburg in 1951.

Seme is best remembered for the 'Native Union' speech of 1911, in which he proclaimed:

> The South African Native Congress is the voice in the wilderness bidding all the dark races of this sub-continent to come together once or twice a year in order to review the past and reject therein all those things which have retarded our progress, the things which poison the springs of our national life and virtue; to label and distinguish the sins of civilisation, and as members of one house-hold to talk and think loudly on our home problems and the solution of them.

SIR SAMUEL FORSTER, 1873-1933
Merton College

WILFRED DAVIDSON CARROL, 1900-41
Merton College

Uncle and nephew - both renowned barristers

Samuel Forster the younger, an Ibo by descent (a people of south-eastern Nigeria), was born on 27 June 1873. He was educated at the Wesleyan Boys' High School in Bathurst, Gambia (now Banjul), and the Church Missionary Society Grammar School in Freetown, Sierra Leone. In 1889 Forester continued his education by travelling to Rhyl in North Wales to attend Epworth College.

The Forster family were clearly wealthy, as is shown by their ability to send their son to an English school, and at the time it was highly unusual for Gambians, unlike Sierra Leoneans, to be educated in Britain. Forster then attended the Liverpool Institute before going up to Merton College, Oxford in 1893 to read law.

He graduated in 1896, and two years later became the first Gambian to qualify as a barrister at the Inner Temple. Returning to Bathurst in 1899, he practised both as a barrister and a solicitor, becoming the most senior Justice of the Peace, and for many years the Leader of the Bar.

Forster held a number of official posts in the 1920s and 1930s as acting colonial registrar, public prosecutor and serving as a Police Magistrate. He served on the Legislative Council as a senior unofficial member from 1906 to 1940.

Forster became a noted member of the Aku (descendants of freed slaves) establishment in Bathurst, likened almost to an aristocracy. The Aku were revered for their intellectual prowess as they were the first ethnic group to acquire Western education in West Africa. Forster founded the Bathurst Reform Club, an exclusive gentlemen's society, in 1928, and remained its president until his death.

In 1927 he was awarded by King George V the status of Member of the Civil Division of the Most Excellent Order of the British Empire (MBE), an Officer of the Order of the British Empire (OBE) in 1930, and he became the first Gambian to receive a knighthood in 1933. He was praised as 'undoubtedly one of the ablest Justices of the Peace that Gambia has ever produced; and as an advocate he had no superior in the colony'.

54

Wilfred Davidson Carrol was born on 13 December 1900 to a prosperous Aku merchant in Bathurst, Gambia. His father, Henry Richmond Carrol, established his store in Russell Street, Bathurst in 1883. The store stocked provisions, hardware, crockery, cotton and general merchandise of all kinds.

Carrol was educated at the Methodist Boys' High School before proceeding to Britain to study at Merton College, taking a second in jurisprudence in 1923 and a second in Civil Law in 1924. While in England he was elected the first president of the West African Students Union.

He trained as a barrister and was called to the Bar in 1924, returning to Gambia in 1925 to establish a practice in Bathurst as a solicitor and barrister. He played a pivotal role in ensuring the implementation of the criminal code and criminal procedure code. Carrol was elected to the Bathurst urban district council in January 1931 for Joloff Town north ward, remaining as a member until his defeat in the 1931 election. In 1933 he was appointed as an Unofficial Member of the Legislative Council.

In spring 1934 Carroll, his brother and others founded the Gambia Echo Syndicate, publishers of the newspaper *The Gambia Echo*, a weekly broadsheet sold for 3d on the streets of Bathurst. Proudly proclaiming that it was 'For King and Country', the paper promoted itself as 'A Journal of Distinctive Policy, The

Merton College

Echo of Deeds and Words, of Politics and Policies in the Gambia, vibrant with Truth'. It was successful in acquiring advertising for major brands from Britain. Carrol was the paper's legal adviser.

Carrol also served on several other public bodies. In poor health from 1938, he died in October 1941. The Banjul city council named a street after him in 1998.

EDUCATIONALISTS

'And then I went off to England to do post-graduate work at Oxford. Now, interestingly, people took me seriously and this is the thing about the great universities anywhere in the world - they're anxious to know what other people are thinking.' Rex Nettleford

RALSTON MILTON (REX) NETTLEFORD, 1933-2010

Oriel College

Scholar, dancer, social commentator, cultural activist and vice chancellor emeritus of the University of the West Indies

Rex Nettleford can best be described as a renaissance man who through his academic and artistic abilities promoted and elevated Jamaican culture to an international platform and audience.

Nettleford was born on 3 February 1933, in the small coastal town of Falmouth, Jamaica, to a mother out of wedlock. Raised by his grandmother, Nettleford grew up in a rural community on the edge of the Cockpit Country, historically the domain of the insurgent Maroons. Nettleford's poor background did not impede him from attending one of Jamaica's most highly regarded secondary school, Cornwall College, in Montego Bay. He was soon recognized as a gifted student with an innate ability as a brilliant dancer. He staged one of his first choreographed dances, 'Boonguzu', whilst at Cornwall College in 1953. The piece illustrated his talent.

Nettleford received a scholarship to the nascent University of the West Indies (UWI) to read for a degree in history. He then became the Jamaican Rhodes Scholar of 1954, attending Oriel College to pursue a postgraduate MPhil degree in politics. His time at Oxford was shared between his studies in politics and choreographing for revues, operas and Shakespearean dramas, working closely with two other Oxford contemporaries, Alan Bennett and Dudley Moore. He also taught Caribbean-influenced dance at meetings of the University Ballet Club. In an interview with the journal *Caribbean Writer*, he described his Oxford days:

> Oxford gave me the opportunity to do a lot because, although I was the choreographer, I was virtually co-director of lots of productions. I remember Dudley Moore, a fellow called Stan Daniels, and I did Aristophanes' *The Birds* to rock music. It was fantastic! I did the choreography and Dudley did the music. That was the last production I did in Oxford itself. Greta and Henry Fowler, the founders of the Little Theatre Movement, were vacationing in Oxford and saw the show. They were so thrilled, they said when I came back home I should work with them. So I went back home two months later and plunged straight into

the pantomime of that year.

The prospect of staying in England did not appeal to Nettleford and he returned to Jamaica to take up a post at UWI in Kingston. Assigned to UWI's extra-mural department by his mentor and founding father of the university, Sir Phillip Sherlock, Nettleford headed the department, eventually nurturing it into the School of Continuing Studies.

His role at the University provided the opportunity for Nettleford to produce groundbreaking research and work. His seminal report on the Rastafarian movement, published in 1961 in collaboration with other noted Caribbean scholars, M. G. Smith and Roy Augier, entitled *The Rastafari Movement in Kingston, Jamaica,* was critically acclaimed and was later cited with helping to give credibility to a social group that had been considered outcasts.

In 1963 Nettleford co-founded the National Dance Theatre Company of Jamaica (NDTC), coinciding with the independence of Jamaica. He performed the multiple roles of artistic director, principal choreographer and, for many years, lead dancer. The Company's style incorporated African religious and folk music traditions into what he termed 'the rhythm of Africa with the melody of Europe'. The company consisted

OXFORD MAIL, FRIDAY, FEBRUARY 14, 1958

UNIVERSITY BALLET CLUB LEARN AFRO CARRIBEAN DANCES

A traditional band plays the blues, and two advanced pupils at the Oxford University Ballet Club's modern theatrical dancing classes start to jive.

Above and below: Rex Nettleford, the instructor, demonstrating a step with two of his pupils.

59

entirely of volunteers, who contributed their expertise on a part-time basis. They toured extensively in Europe and North America and were recognized and hailed as 'one of the cultural jewels of the Caribbean region'.

In 1975 Nettleford received Jamaica's highest non-political order: the Order of Merit. The Institute of Jamaica also acknowledged his contribution to the island cultural heritage, making him a Fellow of the Institute.

Nettleford was selected as vice chancellor of the University of the West Indies in 1996 becoming the first graduate of the university to head the region's premier tertiary level.

To commemorate the centenary of Rhodes Scholarships in the Caribbean in 2003, the Rhodes Trust established the Rex Nettleford Fellowship in Cultural Studies in 2004. The Fellowship is awarded annually in recognition of his cultural pre-eminence and enormous contribution to Caribbean regional development.

In the international arena, Nettleford received some fourteen honorary degrees. He was also made Honorary Fellow of Oriel College. Nettleford served in various leadership capacities on numerous regional and international bodies, including CARICOM and the West Indian Commission, the IDRC, UNESCO, the ILO and the OAS. He was also the recipient of the Zora Neale Hurston–Paul Robeson Award for Outstanding Scholarly Achievement from the National Council for Black Studies, America.

Rex Nettleford died on 2 February 2010 following a heart attack whilst on a speaking engagement in Washington, DC. The Rex Nettleford Foundation was established on 28 May 2010, with a remit 'to support scholars and programmes that promote the strengthening of West Indian society in the areas of social and cultural development through research, community service and intellectual excellence'.

FLORENCE MAHONEY, 1929-PRESENT
St. Hilda's College

Historian and author

'There is only the history of Europeans in Africa. The rest is darkness. And darkness is not the subject of history.'

These were the controversial ideas expressed by Oxford's Regius History Professor, Hugh Trevor-Roper, at a lecture at the University of Sussex in 1963 and then reprinted in *The Listener*. Florence Mahoney was one woman who challenged this preconception: indeed, she insisted, Africa had a rich history, worth studying for its glory and accomplishments. Mahoney is now recognized as one of Gambia's most authoritative historians.

Related to the prominent Sierra Leonean Creole Maxwell family, Mahoney's grandmother's brother, Joseph Renner Maxwell, is believed to be the first African to graduate from Oxford University (see p.81). One of five children, Mahoney was born in 1929 in Bathurst, Gambia to Lenrie Ernest Ingram Peters and Kezia Rosemary. Mahoney attended St. Mary's Anglican primary school and then the Methodist Girls' High School where she passed her Senior Cambridge School Certificate, before moving to St. Elphin's boarding school for girls in Derbyshire, England. She then attended Westfield College - now Queen Mary, University of London - where she received a bachelor's degree with honours in history.

Matriculating at St. Hilda's College, Oxford, Mahoney obtained a postgraduate degree in education. Her PhD in history studies at the School of Oriental and African Studies (SOAS), University of London, made her the first Gambian woman ever to obtain a doctorate. Her achievements were recognized as a great intellectual and physical challenge, especially given the scarcity of collected, catalogued archival material on the Gambian topic she choose to produce her dissertation on. This provided the impetus and the catalyst for Mahoney to work with others in establishing the National Museum in Banjul, Gambia's capital city, in 1973.

Her academic career has seen Mahoney made a Fulbright professor of African History in 1972. She has lectured at Gambia High School, Spelman College, Atlanta, Georgia, and at the Pacific School of Religion in Berkeley, California.

Mahoney has published four books, including the much celebrated *Stories of Senegambia* (1982), *Creole Saga* (2007) and *Gambia Studies* (2008), a collection of essays on some salient aspects of nineteenth-century Gambian history.

LOYISO NONGXA, 1954-PRESENT
Balliol College

The first Black vice chancellor and Principal of Witwatersrand University, South Africa

South Africa's first Black Rhodes scholar, Loyiso Nongxa, sits in prestigious boardrooms and on influential committees as the first Black vice chancellor and Principal of one of South Africa's esteemed institutions - Witwatersrand University. Nongxa's humble upbringing did not impede his start in life, but instead it took him on a journey from herd boy to Oxford-educated mathematician and head of Witwatersrand.

Nongxa was born in Indwe, in the Eastern Cape of South Africa, on 22 October 1954, the youngest of the five children of Tuddie and Tamsanqa Nongxa. His mother, a qualified teacher, chose to stay at home to raise her family; his father was a primary school principal.

Nongxa, like other children in the rural village, tended his father's sheep from the age of five until he went to boarding school at thirteen. Sometimes he missed school but his parents ensured that these were not long enough periods for him to fail or drop out. 'My mother expected us to do well. Failure was not a word in her vocabulary,' says Nongxa. He had a natural aptitude for mathematics, which was discovered in his teens while at Freemantle School. At Healdtown College the lack of qualified teachers in physical science subjects saw a resourceful Nongxa teaching himself. His grasp and ability in these subjects led to him being invited to teach pupils at other schools. Nongxa achieved a distinction as the top mathematics student in South Africa in 1972.

He attended Fort Hare University, taking an active part in university life by playing for the 'Baa-bas', the university's rugby team. Professor Tom van Dyk, his first-year mathematics teacher, spoke of Nongxa's star quality, saying that: 'in [his] thirty years of teaching, Nongxa was one of the best, if not the best student ever. If he scored lower than ninety per cent he wanted to know what was wrong.'

In 1976 Nongxa graduated, with a BSc and MSc *cum laude*. He was awarded the Council Prize for the best performance by an undergraduate student at the university since its inception in 1916.

Nongxa's talent was spotted by Derrick Henderson, a former vice chancellor of Rhodes University, who sat on the Rhodes Scholarship committee. Encouraged to apply for the scholarship by Henderson's wife, Nongxa became

South Africa's first Black Rhodes Scholar in 1978.

On arrival at Oxford, Nongxa refused to do the extra year that was expected from most international postgraduate students, and obtained his DPhil in mathematics in the minimum period of three years. Post-Oxford he spent time at the National University of Lesotho, before being recruited to the University of Natal.

He served as a Professor of Mathematics at the University of the Western Cape. Appointed Dean of the Faculty of Natural Sciences at the University of the Western Cape in 1999, he became Deputy Vice-Chancellor, two years later at Witwatersrand University. Nongxa's momentous appointment as the university's first Black Vice-Chancellor and Principal in May 2003 made history in the university's 85-year existence.

PROFESSOR STUART HALL, 1932-PRESENT
Merton College

Cultural theorist

Stuart Hall has been described as 'Black Britain's leading theorist of Black Britain' by Henry Louis Gates, a renowned academic and Director of the W. E. B. Du Bois Institute for African and African American Research at Harvard University. Hall's achievements span many arenas: as a sociologist, cultural theorist, art critic and political activist.

Hall was born in Jamaica on 3 February 1932; his father was from a lower middle-class family, who went on to work as an accountant in United Food Company. His mother had been adopted by an uncle and aunt from an English expatriate family and raised on a small estate.

Hall's family background and experiences of race, class, colonialism and problems about identity would impact and contribute to shaping his life. He states, 'my mother brought into the family the class aspirations and the estate manners of her adopted relatives and their orientation towards Britishness and the difficulty they experienced in relating to their Jamaican identity.' Hall wanted something different. He felt alienated from this world to which he did not belong and its attitudes towards ordinary Jamaicans. His family was not interested in the popular surge towards self government and independence that were beginning to gain monument on the island.

Hall received a Rhodes Scholarship to study at Merton College, Oxford, arriving in England in 1951, accompanied by his mother, three years after the beginning of post-war Black migration by the so-called 'Windrush generation'.

Feeling excluded from Oxford's white university culture, Hall gravitated instead towards the left and what he describes as 'Oxford's "rebel enclaves", demobbed young veterans, national servicemen, Ruskin College trade unionists, "scholarship boys and girls" from home and abroad'.

His interest in Caribbean politics deepened through his association with many undergraduate and mature West Indian students, becoming increasingly concerned with colonial questions and what was going on 'back home'. Many of the mature West Indian students he knew at Oxford became distinguished senior political and civil servant figures in their countries after independence. Hall cites this generation as particularly significant for Caribbean politics and government: J. O'Neil Lewis was head of the Trinidad Industrial Court under Eric Williams and Trinidad and Tobago's representative in Geneva; Doddridge

Alleyne became Trinidad and Tobago's Ambassador to the United Nations; and William Demas was Secretary-General of CARICOM and President of the Caribbean Development Bank. All of these were close associates of his in his early years at Oxford.

Receiving a second Jamaican scholarship, Hall stayed at Oxford to study for his DPhil, which he later abandoned, on the international theme in the work of the classical American novelist Henry James.

As a graduate student, Hall lived at 12 Richmond Road, which became a focus for political debate among both the Oxford left and Caribbean students. The radical journal *Universities and Left Review,* of which he was a founding member, was produced on his kitchen table in Jericho. He was also the first editor of its successor journal, *New Left Review.*

Hall went to the University of Birmingham initially as a research fellow. Along with Raymond Williams and Richard Hoggart, Hall was instrumental in founding the first cultural research centre in 1964. His appointment in 1968, as director of the new Centre for Contemporary Cultural Studies, and subsequently his groundbreaking work and growing reputation within this field, won him the accolade as 'one of the founding fathers of the academic discipline of cultural studies'.

Hall's influential works - often in essay rather than monograph form - include: *Encoding and Decoding in the Television Discourse; Policing the Crisis; The Hard Road to Renewal: Thatcherism and the Crisis of the Left; New Ethnicities; Cultural Identity, Black Identity and Contemporary Photography and Diaspora; Cultural Representations and Signifying Practices;* and *Visual Culture* among others.

Between 1979 and 1997 Hall was Professor of Sociology at the Open University. After retiring from the Open University, and despite his ill health, he continued to be active within the visual arts field. He became chair of two foundations, Iniva, the Institute of International Visual Arts, and Autograph ABP, an organization formed to promote artists living and working in England but from minority ethnic backgrounds. Hall, with his board members, campaigned for nearly a decade for a permanent home and gallery space for Iniva and Autograph.

Rivington Place, the first newly built public art gallery in London since the Hayward Gallery, was opened on 5 October 2007. Hall hoped that Rivington Place would also provide a platform to showcase artists 'working at the "coalface of difference", chipping away at entrenched positions'. The Library at Rivington Place, named in his honour, houses a substantial collection of catalogues, scholarly articles, periodicals and audio-visual materials focusing on contemporary African, Asian, Latin American and European art, and the work of British artists from different cultural backgrounds.

Hall received the European Cultural Foundation's Princess Margriet Award in 2008, was President of the British Sociological Association and a fellow of the British Academy. He has been awarded honorary degrees from a wide range of universities. He is an Honorary Fellow of Merton College.

CREATIVITY AND LITERATURE

'When I was a student… I remember walking down the streets
in Oxford and coming across a book in a bookstore called
Between Two Cultures: A Study of Immigrants in Britain… I
thought, hell, that's it, isn't it? I'm between two cultures.' Caryl
Phillips in conversation with Pico Iyer

LUSHINGTON WENDELL BRUCE-JAMES
1891-1968
(KNOWN AS BRUCE WENDELL)
Keble College

Composer and concert pianist

Lushington Wendell Bruce-James was born on the island of Antigua on 9 February 1891. His father, Thomas Bruce-James, is described on the birth certificate as a teacher at Music Institution City. Most of his family were educationalists; his uncle, who was a schools inspector, was awarded an MBE (Member of the Order of the British Empire) in the 1930 New Year Honours.

The family moved to British Guiana, now Guyana, while Bruce was a child. The move was a result of his father being headhunted to become headmaster of the Mico Model School. Between the ages of six and eleven Bruce attended Mr Sharpies' school in Georgetown and fifteen he became an organist at Christ Church, Georgetown. After taking the Higher Senior Cambridge examination in 1910, he attended Queen's College where he won the Guiana Scholarship, enabling him to attend Keble College, Oxford, to study classics.

Lushington Wendall Bruce-James (3rd row, centre) matriculation, 1911

The *Daily Chronicle*, Georgetown, British Guiana, Tuesday 7 January 1936, recorded his recollections: 'I went up to Keble because my mother wished me to go into the Church. Music was calling to me with notes even more insistent. I do not believe that there was ever a time when, if I had been psychoanalyzed, it would not have been found that at the back of my mind was the intention to become a musician. But I did not feel a strong vocation to the Church, yet it was the wish of my people, and I decided to follow the course mapped out for me.'

While at Oxford he won second place among all students for the Gaisford Prize, awarded for Greek composition; he was also a contemporary of the then Prince of Wales. In his article 'Oxford in My Time', Bruce states:

> H. A. Lowe, a Barbadian scholar, and I used to go for long walks, conversing in Platonic prose. Lowe won a classical scholarship at Hertford College with a piece of Greek prose so perfect that the examiners commented that it might well have been a lost fragment of Thucydides. C. H. Clarke, another excessively brilliant Barbadian scholar, was at Oxford in my time. He and Hutton-Miles, a West African from Cambridge who used to come over to Oxford to see Clarke, liked to hear me play, and so they had a piano placed in Clarke's room so that whenever I went in to see them they could hear me. There was another West Indian, by the name of Mercier from Jamaica, a Rhodes Scholar, a most charming and cultured fellow, and a great cricketer, who nearly got his blue. Then there were the two Newhams from Barbados, and Nethersole from Jamaica.

During the First World War Bruce was posted to France with the University Corps, Royal Fusiliers. In the same article, he says: 'I joined the 12th and later the 19th Battalion Royal Fusiliers (Public School Corps), and there music pursued me still. I was appointed organist of the battalion, and with certain chosen friends, who represented the choir, used to dodge parades, going off solemnly to almost entirely mythical choir practices.'

Bruce joined the Southern Syncopated Orchestra in 1920; the orchestra had its origins in the New York Syncopated Orchestra, formed in November 1918 under the musical direction of Will Marion Cook. They were the first big band to popularize Black music in Britain, giving a command performance for George V. Bruce was organist and chorus master for their season at the London Kingsway Hall. He devoted himself to deputizing for the leading organists and giving recitals for new organ installations, being particularly successful on the Bernstein Circuit. He invented a new formula for gaining perfection in finger techniques, outlined in the *Melody Maker* (Music in the Kinema) September

23

KEBLE COLLEGE, OXFORD.

Sept. 21. 1905 *withdrawn fo 1907*

1. *Date of application* April 3ᵈ 1905

2. *Surname* Bruce – James.

3. *Christian Name in full* Lushington Wendell ~~Bruce~~

4. *Date of Birth* 9ᵗʰ February 1891. *Baptism* { Church of England. Not known for certain what date –

5. *From what School* Queen's College, B. Guiana.

6. *Name of Parent, Guardian, or other person responsible for the Candidate (specifying whether Father, Guardian, &c., and giving style of address.)*

Mʳˢ Anne Bruce-James (mother)

7. *Address of ditto* 234 New South Road, Georgetown, Demerara.

8. *For what Term and year is entrance desired* Michaelmas Term,

1905 ? 1906

N.B.—If the Candidate has left School, you are requested to state when he left and what he has been doing since

It is specially requested that immediate notice be given to the Warden if any change should take place under Nos. 6, 7, or 8 above, or if it should be no longer intended to send up the Candidate.

1928 article, 'The Ideal Kinema Organ'.

In 1931 Bruce met Mary Clapitt, an English white woman from an impoverished family, while both were employed at the RKO Theatre, known originally as the Leicester Square Theatre, she as an usherette and he as the cinema organist. They married at Hampstead Register Office in 1932 and lived in Golders Green; they had two daughters, Amba and Anne.

In November 1935 Bruce set sail for a concert tour of the West Indies and the United States on the Dutch ship *Colombia*, with a Black Russian opera singer named Madame Zorina. In the *Barbados Advocate* of 2 December 1935, Zorina was described as having 'the most powerful voice of any living soprano', and according to *The Daily Argosy*, of 6 December: 'Madame Zorina, who is of Russian origin, has had a career as striking as her picturesque and commanding personality and includes triumphs in musical art, and heroic suffering and sacrifice during the great War and the Russian revolution. Born in Kiev of a noble Russian family, she embarked upon a dramatic career and when only sixteen years of age was given a role in comic opera. Within a year she married and as the wife of an officer in the Imperial Army she could not appear on the public stage and so she studied medicine and music. Then came the war, in which her husband was killed and on its conclusion, she returned to the concert platform.'

Zorina and Bruce gave concerts in December 1935 in Trinidad, and then moved on to Barbados and British Guiana. In January 1936 they performed in Surinam, where they were afterwards entertained by the governor on his private yacht; they returned to Trinidad, and afterwards proceeded to Venezuela and Tobago.

A number of Guyanese and Barbadian newspapers positively promoted his concerts as 'musical treats'. As well as receiving adulation and praise from the Caribbean press for the concert tour, he also received personal admiration from Rudolph Dunbar, a Guyanese clarinettist; his article in the *Daily Chronicle* on 22 December 1935 was entitled 'Bruce Wendell as I knew him - Your hero and Guyana's illustrious son'. Bruce later became a celebrated pianist, touring in America, Europe and the Caribbean. In June 1939 Bruce was a guest pianist with the Boston Symphony Orchestra. He died on 13 August 1968 in New York, after a long illness.

DAVID UPSHAL, 1967-PRESENT
Corpus Christi

Television executive

Upshal's experience of Oxford is in his own words:

I entered Corpus as a fresh-faced, frightened fresher back in October of 1984 to read Philosophy, Politics and Economics (PPE). All I knew about Oxford when I arrived at Corpus was it would not be like home. Home was Catford, South London, situated at the edge of the city - equidistant, physically and economically, from the grey and brown high-rise housing nightmare of Deptford and the tranquil prosperity of suburban Bromley.

I had attended a large comprehensive school in the middle of a housing estate which was notorious for sending more pupils to prison than university. In my own year of school leavers I was the only one to get into university, while two of my former classmates were detained at Her Majesty's pleasure: one for a stabbing at a football match, the other for a pub brawl which resulted in an attempted murder charge.

Having been made a minor celebrity for becoming the first pupil from my school even to apply, let alone get into, Oxford, I arrived at Corpus with decidedly mixed feelings. *Brideshead Revisited* had just finished its run on television, raising the general perception of Oxford as a bastion of white, upper-class elitism.

Being Black, being from a one parent family, being working-class or just poor, I arrived half fearing I would find *Brideshead* and half hoping I might find something more progressive. I found elements of both.

In my second year, several of my friends decided to run for election for the college's student body, the JCR. Our plan was that we'd take over and revolutionize the place.

Huddled together in Corpus Christi's subterranean beer cellar with our group of plotters one night, I was asked if I'd like to stand. Not much fancying any of the posts on offer, such as secretary, I jokingly said the only post that really appealed was Women's Officer (a newly designated post to represent the interests of female students) and after the laughter died down someone pointed out that there probably ought to be some sort of representation for non-white students. I agreed, but doubted there was much point in being elected to a post that would represent precisely three members of the college.

Someone used the term 'ethnics', which I've always loathed and always challenge. The word 'ethnic', as I'm always at great pains to point out, literally means 'pertaining to race or culture'. Therefore everyone is ethnic. Everyone belongs to a race or culture therefore *everyone* has an ethnicity. It's a gross distortion of the well-intentioned phrase 'ethnic minority', I've always thought, to then describe people of colour exclusively as being 'ethnic'. After I'd finished my short tirade someone said 'you're right - you should tell people that.' It made me think, and I came up with the title of Cultural Relations Officer (or CRO for short) - the role being to cultivate and celebrate the ethnicity of all students regardless of race, creed or colour.

1. To make everyone aware of their own unique cultural identity;

2. To ensure this can be practiced freely without let or hindrance;

3. To encourage college members to accept, appreciate and celebrate each other's ethnic identities;

4. To encourage the recruitment of a wider and more diverse range of ethnic groups to the college so that it better represents all aspects of Britain's population.

The motion to create the new post was passed unanimously by my fellow students. And I was voted into office, unopposed. Apart from making everyone smile about a subject that usually made them feel excruciatingly uncomfortable it also made people think. Underpinning it was a more serious purpose: the recruitment part.

The Oxford University Student Union (OUSU) had begun a Target School scheme, the purpose of which was to reach out to inner-city state schools with no history of Oxford applications and encourage their students to visit and apply for places. I was a huge supporter of this. And I was thrilled when I discovered that my Cultural Relations Officer manifesto was going to be incorporated as a headed paragraph in the Target Schools section of the annual OUSU student handbook. To my knowledge it was the first time the racial make-up of the University population was overtly singled out for mention in official University literature.

After that I discovered that several other Oxford colleges were incorporating the post of Cultural Relations Officer into their Junior Common Rooms. (Indeed when I visited my old college about a decade after I graduated, I was pleasantly surprised when the lodge porter on duty not only greeted me by name but confided that he considered me to be 'the best CRO this college ever had'. He then regaled me with stories about what my successors in the post had got up to. The post, it turned out, was not only going strong, but had clearly expanded considerably since my day.)

Four years after I left Oxford I was working for the BBC on a funky 'yoof TV' series called *Reportage*. As part of a special edition of the show on education, I did a short film about Oxford's Target Schools scheme. I took half a dozen kids from my old comprehensive school to my old college. Cue open-mouthed, working-class kids saying 'I could never dream of going there'; posh Oxford types hosting a dinner party and tour of the place while stressing the very great need

to shake up Oxford and give it a new image; add funky music, some whizz-bang flashes and a healthy dose of swishy sideways camera angles and, well, you get the idea. I was really pleased afterward to learn that three of the kids who went up from my old school felt encouraged enough to apply to Oxford afterwards - and all three of them got in.

*

Now an award-winning television producer and director, Upshal started out at the BBC in 1989 as a production trainee, gaining experience on shows such as *Newsnight*, *Reportage* and *The Late Show* before going on to direct a range of top-quality documentaries including the highly-acclaimed *Vietnam: The Camera at War*.

Upshal produced, directed and narrated the BAFTA and Emmy-nominated series *The Hip Hop Years* and the landmark BBC series *Windrush*, winner of Royal Television Society Award for Best Documentary Series. His other television credits include: *The True Face Of War* (winner of a CINE Special Jury Award, a BANFF World Television Award and a World Medal at the New York Film Festival), *Tony Benn: Free At Last*, *The Funny Life of Richard Pryor* and *The Gospel of Gospel* (featuring Ray Charles, BB King and Al Green).

Joining Lion Television, an independent production company, in 2002 as an Executive Producer, he has overseen two seasons of the Emmy award-winning drama-documentary series *Days That Shook the World* for the BBC and the History Channel in the USA, and he produced *Outbreak Investigation* - a major series of drama-docs on disease epidemics for National Geographic.

Upshal devised and produced the hit BBC2 series *Victorian Farm*, resulting in a long line of follow-up series such as *Victorian Pharmacy, Escape In Time, Edwardian Farm* and *Wartime Farm*

ABENA POKUA ADOMPIM BUSIA, 1953-PRESENT
St. Anne's College, St. Antony's College

Writer, Chair, Department of Women's and Gender Studies, former Director of the Association for the Study of the Worldwide African Diaspora

The daughter of a celebrated Oxford academic and Ghana's President, Kofi Busia (see p.44), Abena has followed in his academic footsteps as a renowned writer, activist, film producer and founder of the Busia Foundation and Busia Foundation International. Born in Accra, Ghana, on 28 April 1953, Abena had her primary education in Ghana, Holland and Mexico before her family was exiled from Ghana, finally settling in Oxford, where she grew up in a little village twelve miles outside the city.

Abena continued her primary education at Standlake Church of England Primary School before attending Witney Grammar School, where she and her cousin Afua were the only Black children at the school; she completed her secondary education at Headington Girls' School, Oxford.

Abena matriculated at St. Anne's College to read for a BA in English Language and Literature in 1976, taking her postgraduate degree and Doctorate in Social Anthropology (Race Relations) at St. Antony's College in 1984.

> There was an Africa Society to which I belonged. I ended up actually becoming, first, secretary and then president of the Africa Society. At my own college at Oxford, there was another Ghanaian who became quite a well known actress called Muriel Odunton. She became quite famous in England for a situation-comedy called *Mixed Blessings*, then moved to the United States, and Hugh Quarshie, at Christ Church, was in the same year.

As a graduate student, Abena was much more conscious of her father's legacy at Oxford than she had been as an undergraduate. Recalling a touching incident, Abena tells of when she was going to receive her MA at a graduation ceremony:

> I am hurrying through St. Giles down from my college to the Sheldonian Theatre when I see one of the most distinguished anthropology professors, Professor Edwin Ardener in his gown, he's clearly going to the same ceremony.
> He falls into step with me and we're making conversation. I knew

who he was by sight. But really, I had had very little contact with him. As we are going to the examinations school I innocently ask him, 'Who are you going to the ceremony for?' And he stops in his tracks, looks at me like in utter surprise and says, 'the daughter of one of my former colleagues, now deceased, is getting her master's degree. Who do you think I'm going to the ceremony for?' I was so stunned. I had no idea.

An accomplished and award winning writer, Abena is the co-editor of *Theorizing Black Feminisms*, and co-director of the groundbreaking Women Writing Africa Project, a multi-volume collective publishing project which was two decades in the making. Abena lectures and publishes widely on African Diaspora literature and culture and curriculum transformation for race and gender. She has published two volumes of poems: *Testimonies of Exile* and *Traces of a Life*. Her poetry has also been published in various magazines and anthologies in West Africa, North America and Europe. She has also contributed chapters on Black women's writing, Black feminist criticism and African literature to countless books and journals.

She was the co-executive producer and consultant with her sister, Akosua Busia, for the documentary films: *The Prof, A Man Remembered: The Life, Vision and Legacy of Dr. Kofi Abrefa Busia* and *Portrait of a First Lady: A Tribute to Mrs Naa-Morkor Busia*.

Abena is currently Chair of the Department of Women's and Gender Studies, an Associate Professor in the Departments of Literatures in English and Comparative Literature and Associate Director of the Centre for African Studies at Rutgers, the State University of New Jersey at New Brunswick. She also serves as Board Chair of the African-Women's Development Fund-USA.

CARYL PHILLIPS, 1958-PRESENT
The Queen's College

Author and playwright

'It was whilst I was in the United States that I made the "discovery" that it was possible for a Black person to become, and sustain a career as, a writer.' Describing what felt like an explosion in his head after reading Richard Wright's book *Native Son*, Phillips recognized this as a crucial moment in his desire to become a writer.

Born in the small Caribbean island of St. Kitts to Malcolm and Lillian Phillips on 13 March 1958, Phillips came to England as a twelve-week-old infant. Growing up in Leeds, Yorkshire, in predominately white working-class areas, his education was mainly at white middle-class schools.

Phillips won a place at The Queen's College, Oxford, where he read English, graduating in 1979. At Oxford, he was, he recalls 'less sure of myself, there was a lot of pressure to conform to an Oxford ideal as I noticed other students who had also come from Yorkshire losing their accents within three weeks of being at the university.' At the suggestion of his friend, an African-American Rhodes Scholar, Emile Leroi Wilson, he resolved to 'plug into Black life'. Finishing a tutorial he would take a train from Oxford to Paddington and head for Ladbroke Grove to a pub that was crowded with Black people to soak up the culture and where he would find himself engaged in lengthy debates.

At Oxford he acquired a love for theatre, directing numerous plays and spending a summer working as a stagehand at the Edinburgh Festival. Retreating back to Edinburgh after his finals, a city where he said 'he found peace, and lived for a year, Phillips produced his first play *Strange Fruit*, which was taken up and produced by the Crucible Theatre in Sheffield. He wrote two further plays, *Where There Is Darkness* and *Shelter*, when he moved back to London. Both plays were staged at the Lyric Theatre in Hammersmith.

The inspiration for his first novel, *The Final Passage*, was motivated by his first visit back to St. Kitts; published five years later, it won the Malcolm X Prize for Literature. After his second book, *A State of Independence*, Phillips took a year-long journey round Europe, to define what Europe meant to him and his own sense of identity. Starting in Morocco and finishing in Moscow, his observations resulted in his collection of essays, *The European Tribe*, which won the 1987 Martin Luther King Memorial Prize.

In the late 1980s and early 1990s Phillips divided his time between England

and St. Kitts while working on his subsequent novels, *Higher Ground* and *Cambridge*. For *Cambridge*, Phillips received the 1992 Sunday Times Young Writer of the Year Award.

While at Amherst College in Massachusetts, as the youngest English tenured professor in America, Phillips produced what is arguably his most acclaimed novel, *Crossing the River*. It won the James Tait Black Memorial Prize and was shortlisted for the Booker Prize. He has written extensively for radio, television and film, producing the screenplay for Ismail Merchant's 2001 film adaptation of V. S. Naipaul's *The Mystic Masseur*.

Phillips is currently a professor of English at Yale University. He was made an elected fellow of the Royal Society of Literature in 2000, and an elected fellow of the Royal Society of Arts in 2011 and is also an Honorary Fellow of The Queen's College, Oxford.

OTHER NOTABLE GRADUATES

Joseph Renner Maxwell (1857-1901) was a controversial figure thanks to the publication of his book *The Negro Question*. Born into the very prominent Sierra Leonean Creole Maxwell family on 12 November 1857, Maxwell was the first son of Thomas Maxwell, a garrison chaplain to British troops at Cape Coast in the British Gold Coast colony, and the grand uncle of Florence Mahoney (see p.61).

Educated at the Church Missionary Society (CMS) Grammar School in Freetown, Maxwell entered Merton College on 14 October 1876, aged nineteen to read for a BA, which he took in 1879 followed by his Masters in 1883 and Bachelor of Civil Law (BCL) in 1884. He is believed to be the first African to graduate from Oxford University. He was a student at Lincoln's Inn in 1878 and was called to the Bar on 17 November 1880.

Maxwell wrote happily of his time at Oxford, stating, 'I was not subjected to the slightest ridicule or insult on account of my colour or race from any of my fellow students.' In West Africa, by contrast, he said he had met with sarcasm from Englishmen with regard to his physical appearance.

Maxwell practised as a barrister in the Gold Coast, now Ghana, and had a successful law firm. He was appointed Queen's Advocate to the Gambia Colony in 1883. Four years later he was appointed as was the Chief Magistrate of the

Joseph Renner Maxwell (centre)

colony. He was also an ex officio member of the Legislative and Executive Councils. He married an English woman, Ada Mana Beale of Richmond.

In 1891 he published his book entitled *The Negro Question or, hints for the physical improvement of the Negro race, with special reference to West Africa.* The book proposes the controversial theory of miscegenation - marriage between Black Africans and Caucasians to dilute and therefore improve the physical appearance of the Negro race - although he argues there is no mental or academic inferiority on the part of the Negro. It maybe concluded that the treatment he received in West Africa led him to promulgate this self-hating theory. He wrote: 'I am a Negro of pure descent, I have travelled… been educated at Oxford… but I must confess with regret that, except the Chinese, I have never seen another race approaching, even within a measurable distance, the Negro in ugliness.' In 1897 he resigned from his office on the grounds of ill health, and retired to England. He died at sea on returning to West Africa in 1901.

*

Arthur Eardley Maxwell Gibson was the eldest son of Zachariah Thomas Gibson, a solicitor of Sierra Leone. Maxwell Gibson was educated at Fourah Bay Missionary College and matriculated at Wadham College, Oxford, where he achieved a third in law in 1897 and a third in his BCL in 1898.

A brief mention in the college gazette notes that he 'did his best to take part in all College activities', that he was 'a loyal member of the College to the last' and 'maintained Wadham's legal reputation at the West African Bar'. It also mentions that he had been 'a pupil of Lord Birkenhead', i.e. F. E. Smith, Wadham (matriculated 1891), later Lord Chancellor, 'who not only instructed him in Law, but also saved him from drowning, when, with childlike confidence he plunged into deep water before he had learned to swim'. The college archivist remarks that 'the whole entry seems a shade patronising, but perhaps I am reading that into it. Birkenhead, of course, was much given to elaborating stories, so I would have my reservations about this.'

Gibson was called to the Bar in 1898 at Gray's Inn. He contributed to the *Journal of the African Society* of October 1903 an article on 'Slavery in West Africa'.

*

A barrister of great distinction and the third President of Trinidad and Tobago, **Arthur Napoleon Raymond Robinson, SC, OCC, TC** was born on 16 December 1926 in Calder Hall, Tobago. Robinson attended the school where his father was principal, Tobago's Castara Methodist School. He achieved two firsts which enabled him to progress in his education: the first Bowles Scholarship to Bishop's High School in 1939, and the first House Scholarship from Bishop's High School in 1942.

Robinson continued his studies in Tobago, gaining admission to the Bachelor of Law degree at London University as an external student in 1949. He left for the United Kingdom in 1951, to enter the Inner Temple, where he passed the Bar final examinations in 1953. That same year he was admitted to St. John's College, Oxford, where with in two years he obtained a good second class honours degree in Philosophy, Politics and Economics.

He practised as a barrister-at-law in Trinidad and Tobago, and was in the Chambers of Sir Courtney Hannays from 1957 to 1961. A founding member and deputy political leader of the People's National Movement (PNM), he was the first Minister of Finance after independence and was responsible for the restructuring of the country's financial institutions and the reform of financial and monetary policy.

Robinson was Prime Minister of Trinidad and Tobago between 1986 and 1991 and President from 1997 to 2003. He is internationally recognized for his proposal that eventually led to the founding of the International Criminal Court.

Awarded a Knighthood of Honour and of Merit by the Ecumenical Foundation of the Knights of St. John for 'exceptional achievements and unselfish support of humanity', Robinson is also an Honorary Fellow of St. John's College, Oxford.

*

The first person to write about Africans in the works of Shakespeare was **Professor Eldred Durosimi Jones,** in his ground breaking book, *Othello's Countrymen: the African in English Renaissance Drama*. Published in 1965, it garnered Jones accolades and established his reputation in the field.

Jones was born on 5 January 1925

The Autobiography of Arthur N R Robinson
In The Midst Of It

and educated at the Sierra Leone Grammar School and Fourah Bay College. His parents were Sierra Leonean Creoles. He matriculated at Corpus Christi College in 1950, and in his autobiographical *The Freetown Bond* evokes the atmosphere of the college:

> In Evelyn Waugh's *Brideshead Revisited*, Charles Ryder's cousin advises his young relation against taking rooms in the quad of his college. My rooms in my second year in Corpus Christi College were in the Pelican Quad, within a few paces of the hall, chapel and junior common room but, unlike Ryder's cousin, I never felt either besieged or misused by other undergraduates always popping in and out of my rooms, depositing their gowns after chapel and otherwise disturbing my peace. Friends did after dinner in hall occasionally drop in for coffee as I did on others in this small college...

Jones' career spanned academic, political and civic achievement with a lifelong commitment to African culture. His commitment saw him establish and become editor of *African Literature Today* for 35 years. The journal played a crucial role in the consolidation and dissemination of African literary studies.

A Fellow of the Royal Society of Arts, Jones is a recipient of the Royal Society of Arts Silver Medal, Honorary Fellow of Corpus Christi College, Oxford, and joint winner, with his wife Marjorie Jones, of the African Studies Association UK's Distinguished Africanist Award.

*

Ethelred Nathaniel Jones was a Sierra Leonean pioneer - with the sole aim of improving the lives of his people and the unity of his country. Jones was one of the most prominent leaders in pre-independence Sierra Leone. He founded one of the first political parties, a savings bank, a newspaper and an African church.

Born at Gloucester, in the Mountain District of Freetown, on 28 June 1884, Jones went to Fourah Bay College where he graduated with a BA. Jones wanted to preach and teach among the people of Sierra Leone, deciding to take holy orders, much to the dismay of his father, who wanted his son's academic abilities to take him into medicine. Jones matriculated in 1921 at Wycliffe Hall, a small evangelical theological college situated in Banbury Road, its staff and student body totalling only fifteen people at the time. The Rev. H. B. Gooding was the principal at the time (see p.33). Jones read theology and philosophy.

At Oxford he encountered the sour taste of racial prejudice. An Anglican bishop in a sermon had appealed for candidates for ordination; Jones wrote

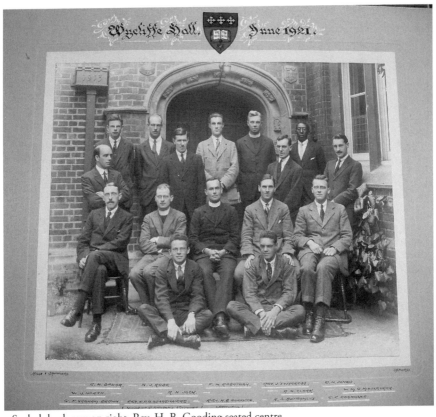

Sankoh back row on right, Rev. H. B. Gooding seated centre

offering himself for the ministry. The response from the bishop stated that 'on no account would [he] lay his hands on a black man's head'. Not only did this response shock him but it would later lead him to start using his original Temne name. In 1923 he was ordained a deacon by the Bishop of Peterborough, who reportedly wore white gloves in protection against his 'blackness', which he removed after the service.

Adopting the name Lamina Sankoh, he returned home in 1924 and was appointed curate of Holy Trinity Church, a post he held until 1927. During his curacy, he also lectured in logic at Fourah Bay College. Disillusioned with the Church in Sierra Leone, Sankoh resigned his curacy and returned to Britain to gain a postgraduate qualification in education at Oxford. A year later he travelled to the United States, where he taught at various Historically Black Colleges and Universities.

The 1930s found Sankoh back in Britain and active in the West African Students

Union (WASU), a political pressure group agitating for self-government. He was also a regular contributor to the *WASU Journal*, later becoming its editor.

Returning to Sierra Leone in the early 1940s Jones embarked on a political and civic career, becoming a councillor for Freetown City Council, president of the Freetown Adult Education Committee, establishing a Penny Savings Bank, a newspaper in Freetown called *The African Vanguard*, and an African church where theology and philosophy were relatively free of Western influences.

He founded the People's Forum and the People's Party in 1948, which eventually became the party known today as the Sierra Leone People's Party. Sankoh died in 1954. He has a prominent street named after him in downtown Freetown.

∗

A number of Ghanaian Presidents have been educated at Oxford University. These include **Edward Akufo-Addo**, who attended Achimota School in Accra, from which he won a scholarship to study mathematics, politics and philosophy at St. Peter's College, Oxford. He qualified as a barrister at the Middle Temple, London, and returned to the Gold Coast, now Ghana. He was one of the 'Big

Six' leaders of the United Gold Coast Convention political party, which fought for Ghana's independence. He became Chief Justice and then President of Ghana from 1970 until 1972. Addo died in 1979 of natural causes.

Ghana's second President **John Kofi Agyekum Kufuor** was born in Kumasi and educated at Osei Tutu boarding school and Prempeh College, graduating at the top of his class. He enrolled at Lincoln's Inn, London, and at the age of 22 was called to the Bar in 1961

On the advice of friend and former Oxford graduate, President Busia, Kufuor matriculated at Exeter College, where he gained a BA in Philosophy, Politics and Economics in 1964. In accordance with Oxford traditions, he was subsequently confirmed with the Master's degree by the University.

One of the founding members of the Progress Party (PP) in 1969, the Popular Front Party (PFP) in 1979 and the New Patriotic Party (NPP), Kufuor was twice elected as a member of parliament and was a deputy foreign minister in Kofi Abrefa Busia's government. Winning elections in December 2000, Kufour was sworn in as president on 7 January 2001. He has been honoured with numerous awards, including the Face-of-Good-Governance Award, Chatham House Prize, the Climate Change Award and the World Food Program's Global Ambassador against Hunger.

To celebrate his leadership in Ghana and to mark Ghana's fiftieth Independence Anniversary, the Kufuor Biographical Project presented a very generous gift to Exeter College to establish a scholarship. The Kufuor Scholarship (linked to the Clarendon Award) is awarded to a top Ghanaian student to undertake a graduate degree at the College.

*

Sir Hugh Worrell Springer was a noted educator, politician, parliamentarian and Governor General of Barbados. Springer, educated at the prestigious Harrison College, achieved a 1931 Barbados Scholarship in classics. The scholarship qualified him for entry to Hertford College, Oxford, where he read Greek, gaining a BA degree in 1936 and an MA degree in 1944. He studied law at the Inner Temple, London and was called to the Bar in 1938.

THE RIGHT EXCELLENT
SIR HUGH
WORRELL SPRINGER

Truly
a
Gentleman

Kean Springer

Returning to Barbados, Springer practised as a barrister for almost ten years before leaving to take up the post of Registrar of the newly created University College of the West Indies in Jamaica from 1947 to 1962. He held numerous professional and political positions including Director of the Institute of Education, Member of the House of Assembly, General Secretary of the Barbados Labour Party and Acting Governor and Commander-in-Chief of Barbados. He was elected an Honorary Fellow of Hertford College in 1974 and a Senior Visiting Fellow at All Souls. His portrait hangs in All Souls Dining Hall. Sir Hugh Springer died in 1994. He was named one of Barbados' ten National Heroes in 1998.

*

The first Black person to be elected president of the prestigious Oxford Union in 1942, **Sir James Cameron Tudor** was another distinguished Barbadian politician and educator, noted as one of the best political orators to have graced the Caribbean.

Matriculating at The Queen's College, Tudor was a contemporary of British politician Sir Roy Jenkins. After graduating, he taught for a while in Barbados and British Guiana. He was first elected in 1951 to the Barbados House of Assembly.

A founding member of the Democratic Labour Party, Tudor was instrumental in securing independence for Barbados, made possible through his relationships with key individuals in the British establishment. He earmarked 30 November,

St. Andrew's Day, as the date for Barbados to achieve political independence.

After the 1966 general election Tudor was elevated to Deputy Prime Minister and Minister of State for Caribbean and Latin American Affairs. He held the appointment as High Commissioner to the United Kingdom and served briefly as Permanent Representative to the United Nations. He was also Head of the Mission of Barbados to the European Mission. He died in July 1995.

'Oxford will always have its history - for better or for worse. It will always be regarded as a place steeped in privilege, slightly removed from the real world by its dizzy academic altitude (and perhaps attitude too). But all I'd say to anyone is there's no reason why that should exclude us. And, judging by the contents of this book, perhaps that has been the case for far longer than most people imagine'. - **David Upshal**

FURTHER READING

Agyeman-Duah, Ivor, *Between Faith and History: A Biography of J. A. Kufuor.* Trenton, NJ: Africa World Press, 2003

Busia, Abena P. A.; James, Stanlie M.;, *Theorizing Black Feminisms: The Visionary Pragmatism of Black Women.* New York: Routledge 1993

Busia, Abena P. A., *Testimonies of Exile.* Trenton, NJ: Africa World Press, 1990.

Busia, Abena P. A., *Traces of a Life: A Collection of Elegies and Praise Poems.* Banbury: Ayebia Clarke Publishing Ltd, 2008.

Busia, Kofi Abrefa, *The Challenge of Africa.* New York: Praeger, 1962.

Busia, Kofi Abrefa, *Africa in Search of Democracy.* New York: Praeger, 1967.

Butcher, Margaret Just, *The Negro in American Culture: based on materials left by Alain Locke.* New York: A. A. Knopf, 1972.

Carter, Gwendolen Margaret; Morgan, E. Philip, *From the frontline: speeches of Sir Seretse Khama.* Stanford: Hoover Institution Press, 1980.

Danso-Boafo, Alex Kwaku, *The Political Biography of Dr Kofi Abrefa Busia.* Accra: Ghana Universities Press, 1996.

Dutfield, Michael, *A marriage of Inconvenience: The Persecution of Ruth and Seretse Khama.* London: Unwin Hyman, 1990.

Franklin Bowes, Ann, *From Your Daddy.* London: Athena, 2006

Harris, Leonard; Molesworth, Charles, *Alain L. Locke: the Biography of a Philosopher.* Chicago: University of Chicago Press, 2010.

Hoyos, F. A., *Grantley Adams and the Social Revolution: the story of the movement that changed the pattern of West Indian society.* London: Macmillan, 1974.

Hoyos, F. A., *Tom Adams: A Biography.* London: Macmillan Carribean, 1988

Jones, Eldred Durosimi, *The Freetown Bond: A Life Under Two Flags.* New York: James Currey 2012

Locke, Alain, *The new Negro.* New York: Simon & Schuster, 1925.

Mahoney, Florence, *Creole Saga: the Gambia's liberated African Community in the nineteenth century.* 2006.

Mahoney, Florence, *Stories of Senegambia.* Pretoria: Government Printer, South Africa, 1982.

Mashamaite, Moss, *The Second Coming: the Life and Times of Pixley Ka Isaka Seme, the Founder of the ANC.* Pretoria: Chatworld Publishers, 2011.

Maxwell, Joseph Renner, *The Negro Question or Hints for the Physical Improvement of the Negro.* London: T. F. Unwin, 1892.

Morley, David; Chen, Kuan-Hsing, *Stuart Hall: Critical Dialogues in Cultural Studies.* New York: Routledge, 1996.

Nettleford, Rex M., *Inward Stretch, Outward Reach: A Voice from the Carribean.* Basingstoke: Macmillan, 1993.

Nettleford, Rex, *Norman Washington Manley and the New Jamaica: Selected Speeches and Writings 1938-68.* Trinidad: Longman Carribean, 1971

Nettleford, Rex M.; Hall, Kenneth O., *Rex N: Rex Nettleford – Selected Speeches.* Kingston: Ian Randle, 2006.

Phillips, Caryl, *Strange Fruit.* Ambergate: Amber Lane Press, 1981.

Phillips, Caryl, *The European Tribe.* New York: Vintage Books, 2000.

Rive, Richard; Couzens, Tim, *Seme: the Founder of the ANC.* Trenton, NJ: Africa World Press, 1993.

Robinson, Arthur Napoleon Raymond, *A. N. R. Robinson in the Midst of it: the Autobiography of former Prime minister and Former president of the Republic of Trinidad and Tobago.* London: Hansib Publications, 2012.

Rosiji, Gbemi, *Lady Ademola*: Portrait of a Pioneer. Lagos: EnClair Publishers Limited, 1996.

Ryan, Selwyn D., *Eric Williams: the Myth and the Man.* Kingston: University of the West Indies Press, 2009.

Sherlock, Philip Manderson, Sir, *Norman Manley.* London: Macmillan, 1980

Springer, Kean H. W., *Truly a Gentleman: The Right Excellent Sir Hugh Worrell Springer.* Kingston; Miami: Ian Randle Publishers, 2008.

Upshal, David; Ogg, Alex, *The Hip-Hop years: A History of Rap.* New York: Fromm International, 2001.

Williams, Eric, *Capitalism and Slavery.* London: Deutsch, 1964.

Williams, Eric, *Inward Hunger: The Education of a Prime Minister.* London: Deutsch, 1969.

Williams, Susan, *The Colour bar; The Triumph of Seretse Khama and His Nation.* London: Penguin UK, 2007.

General:

Green, Jeffrey, *Black Edwardians: Black People in Britain 1901-1914.* New York: Frank Cass Publishers, 1998.

Méndez, Serafín Méndez; Cueto, Gail A., *Notable Carribeans and Carribean Americans: A Biographical Dictionary.* Westport: Greenwood Publishing Group, 2003.

Schaeper, Thomas J.; Schaeper, Kathleen, *Cowboys into Gentlemen: Rhodes Scholars, Oxford, and the Creation of an American Elite.* Oxford; New York: Berghahn Books, 1998.

Sandiford, Keith A. P, *A Black Studies Primer: Heroes and Heroines of the African Diaspora.* London: Hansib Publications, 2008.

Zeigler, Philip, *Legacy: Cecil Rhodes, The Rhodes Trust and Rhodes Scholarships.* New Haven; London: Yale University Press, 2008.

ACKNOWLEDGEMENTS & CREDITS

I must express a thank you to all the people and scholars who contributed their time, knowledge and expertise to enable the creation of this book, in particular, their support and encouragement and enthusiasm for the subject matter and individual scholars.

I would like to extend a warm thank you to all the following:

University of Oxford College Archivists for accessing information and assisting with photographic images and clearances: in particular, Mr. Clifford Davies, Wadham College; Mr. Robert Petre, Keble College; Mr. Andrew Mussell, Lincoln College, Dr. Robin Darwall-Smith, Magdalen College, who was always available at the click of a mouse to answered my constant email queries and questions; Mr. Michael Riordan, St. John's College; and Julian Reed, Merton College. Additional archivists: Bill Muller, Archivist, Townsville Grammar School; Tom McCutchon, Public Services Specialist, Columbia University rare books and manuscripts; Susan G. Hamson, Curator of Manuscripts & University Archivist, Columbia University; Joellen Elbashir, Curator of Manuscripts, Moorland Spingarn Research Center, Howard University; Tameside Local Studies and Archives Centre, Central Library; Hassoum Ceesay, senior official, National Centre for Arts and Culture, Banjul, Gambia; Peter H. Weis, Archivist, Northfield Mount Hermon Archives; Lynn Meyers, State Library of Queensland.

Oxford University staff: Jeremy Coote, Curator, Pitt Rivers Museum and Christopher Morton, Curator of Photographs and Manuscript, Pitt Rivers Museum; Clare Woodcock, Head of Information, Public Affairs Unit; Dr. Julia Walworth, The Fellow Librarian, Merton College; The Warden and Fellows of Merton College, Oxford; Simon Lloyd, Bursar, Hertford College; Simon Bailey, Keeper of the Archives, Bodleian Library; and Vince O'Connor, academic registrar, Wycliffe College.

The local historians and family members who provided invaluable information: Peter Vernier; Michael and Margaret Wortley; Ann Bowes, daughter of Lushington Wendall Bruce-James for also welcoming me into her home and her time in talking about her father; Rachel Manley and Ainsley Henriques, Michael Manley Foundation; Erica Williams, Eric Williams Memorial Collection.

Ian Wishart, The Guyana Queen's College Association; His Excellency Laleshwar KN Singh, CCH, The High Commissioner for Guyana in the United Kingdom; Antiona Joseph, Information Officer, High Commission of Antigua and Barbuda; Mr. Nigel Skinner, Editor, *Tameside Reporter*, Tristram Wyatt and Robert Taylor.

On behalf of Signal Books, thanks to Michelle Fisher, Fiona Macgregor and Brenda Stones.

Picture Credits

INDEX